To Anne much love
[signature] 19-7-2018

Loneliness Knows My Name

John O'Brien OFM

[signature] John O'Brien

Other books by the author

Catch the Wind
Return to Gethsemane
My one Friend is Darkness
Rachel's Tears and Mary's Song
Love Rescue Me
Cry Me a River
Therese and the Little Way of Love and Healing
Clare of Assisi: A living Flame of Love
Waiting for God: From trauma to Healing
With Thee Tender is the Night

To all who suffer loneliness and those we have lost.

To Pope Francis, who teaches us to meet the broken with love and kindness, to bind their wounds.

"The human spirit can endure in sickness,
but as for a broken spirit, who can bear it."
(Prov 18:14)

"...God himself will be with them as their God.
He will wipe away every tear from their eyes,
and there will be no more death or mourning or crying
or pain for the former things will have passed away."
(Rev 21:3f)

Contents

Introduction

Many people today take their lives. Loneliness and depression are very real. St. Teresa of Calcutta (+1997) said that the biggest disease of today is not leprosy or tuberculosis, but rather the feeling of being unwanted. Being unwanted, feeling unloved and unlovable are the hallmarks of loneliness. Yet when one person speaks out about their experience this helps break the circle and people feel empowered to struggle.

The 2013 film 'Gravity' is set in Space. It is about two characters in Space and their fight for survival when disaster strikes. Matt Kowalski (George Clooney) is a confident, buoyant astronaut, accompanied by Dr. Ryan Stone (Sandra Bullock), a passive medical engineer on her first mission in Space. In one of the most poignant scenes of the film Dr. Stone expresses her sadness and fear in the looming face of death: "No one will mourn for me. No one will pray for my soul. Will you mourn for me? Will you pray for me? I mean I'd pray for myself, but I've never prayed – nobody ever taught me how."

The first step in prayer is to listen to what is in our hearts and put words on the experience, then address the words to God. This for many is the most frightening step – when we feel unwanted then we feel as if we do not like ourselves and becomes ashamed of what is inside us. Yet it can be done. Eric Clapton had such a moment. Once when he was in despair of his addiction to alcohol and drugs he cried out to God and then he felt as if there was a gentle feminine presence in the room. He wrote 'Holy Mother' to express his prayer and the sense of a gentle presence:

> Holy Mother, where are you?
> Tonight I feel broken in two.
> I've seen the stars fall from the sky.
> Holy mother, can't keep from crying.
>
> Oh I need your help this time,
> Get me through this lonely night.
> Tell me please which way to turn
> To find myself again.

Holy mother, hear my prayer,
Somehow I know you're still there.
Send me please some peace of mind;
Take away this pain.

Vincent Van Gogh was someone else who knew loneliness and depression. At one stage he left institutional religion because he did not fit in. In the Borinage in Belgium he shared the lot of the miners and their poverty, but he was not accepted for ministry. Later he wrote to Theo his brother: "That does not keep me from having a terrible need of – shall I say the word – religion. Then I go out at night and paint the stars."[1] Van Gogh was seeking new symbols to give expression to his religious vision. He saw his art as doing this. In his painting 'The Olive Trees' (1889) he tried to use art to express his feelings and the feelings of Jesus in Gethsemane (see Mk 14:32-42). When he painted this work he was in mental anguish and emotional turmoil. He always identified with the poverty, loneliness and rejection of Jesus, the suffering servant. This gave him strength. Van Gogh always hungered for the infinite God to heal his pain. In the Starry Night (1890) Van Gogh shows the starry sky, there is the village scene, the cypress tree and the sky. The village contains elements from Vincent's memory of Holland. Vincent said "When all sounds cease, God's voice is heard under the stars" (At the Edge of Eternity, p. 172). The sky is full of radiant light and pulsating rhythms. Van Gogh once wrote to Theo about his association of the constellation of the night sky with eternity and the divine love of God, and he says: "The moon is still shining, and the sun and the evening star, which is a good thing – and they also speak of the love of God and make one think of the words: 'So, I am with you always, even to the end of the world'" (Edge of Eternity, p 174). Vincent put all his love into his paintings and it was his dream that people would feel that love and be healed.

In looking at a work of Van Gogh or any other painter we can find an expression of our feelings and being enraptured by the painting feel we

---

[1] see Kathleen Powers Erickson, At Eternity's Gate: The Spiritual Vision of Vincent Van Gogh (Grand Rapids: 1998), p. 148.

are not alone. Similarly with reading – we read to know we are not alone (C.S. Lewis). This can be a natural opening to prayer. As we remain in silence we are drawn out of ourselves into the world of the artist. As we remain in silence beholding God and his words, Jesus and the saints (the artists of the Infinite) we are drawn into love. The quiet still voice of love reaches us across the silence and we become one with the beloved. Our main fault is not to doubt God (we say we do!) but to doubt ourselves and feel unworthy. In Luke 5:8 when Jesus calls Peter, Peter says "Go away from me, Lord, I am a sinful man". Our big problem is to be able to remain silent before the Infinite and stay still. We run miles not to be alone with ourselves. This work is a shared prayer helping us put words on our experience of loneliness and enables us to stand in silence before the 'mercy seat'. Clapton and Van Gogh found ways to articulate their fears and loneliness and they can inspire us with our fears and doubts, loneliness and heartaches.

We finish with the following story of the prophet Elijah from the Book of Kings:

> The encounter with God
> There he went into a cave and spent the night there. Then the word of Yahweh came to him saying, 'What are you doing here, Elijah?' He replied, 'I am full of jealous zeal for Yahweh Sabaoth, because the Israelites have abandoned your covenant, have torn down your altars and put your prophets to the sword. I am the only one left, and now they want to kill me.' Then he was told, 'Go out and stand on the mountain before Yahweh.' For at that moment Yahweh was going by. A mighty hurricane split the mountains and shattered the rocks before Yahweh. But Yahweh was not in the hurricane. And after the hurricane, an earthquake. But Yahweh was not in the earthquake. And after the earthquake, fire. But Yahweh was not in the fire. And after the fire, a light murmuring sound. And when Elijah heard this, he covered his face with his cloak and went out and stood at the entrance of the cave.
>
> (1 Kings 19:9-13)

Elijah had been banished by Queen Jezebel and he feels broken. The first step is when he rests and eats at the command of God (1 Kings 19:1-9). Then he goes to Mount Horeb to pray. Here Elijah hears the hurricane and the earthquake (the traditional symbols of the appearance of divine, see Exodus 19:6-19), yet Yahweh (God) was not in any of these. Then he hears a gentle 'light, murmuring sound'. He knows God is here. The translation for the Hebrew contains a paradox, it reads "the sound of fine silence"[2] or "the gentle voice of silence". This is different from the Sound of Silence by Simon and Garfunkel (1964). Here the gentle voice of silence is the Presence of God who is love. We are like Elijah, we must wait to hear the gentle voice of love in our hearts. That is the cure for our loneliness – God is our health.

[2] see S. Prickett, Theology 80 (1977), 403-410,
    R. Coote, "Yahweh recalls Elijah" in Traditions and Transformation (Winona Lake: 1981), p. 118f.

Chapter One

Loneliness knows my name:

Mother (now Saint) Teresa (+1997) said that the biggest disease today is not leprosy or tuberculosis but rather the feeling of being unwanted. This expresses itself in deep loneliness, pain and isolation. Young men, in particular, feel this pain but for social reasons fail to articulate their pain and so many take their lives. Women, as a rule, are better at talking about emotions than men. This does not mean however that women don't suffer. Their pain should not be trivialised. This feeling of being unwanted, this feeling of loneliness comes from many sources. Rejection, bullying and abuse (whether it be psychological, physical, sexual, religious etc.) lead people to the belief that they are somehow worthy of this treatment and they internalise the message. How many people leave abusive relationships to end up in yet another abusive relationship. The church one time was seen as a place of acceptance – however even here there was bullying and sexual abuse. I know this from experience. For many the church is closed to them because of abuse and the consolation of God's love in Jesus has become something remote and distant. The hurt is too great, the fear and self-loathing too strong and the loneliness and the feeling of non-acceptance too overwhelming. In recent years the church has begun to make efforts to tackle this great failure.

Others find rejection in schools. Schools, for many, were places of brutality and beatings. Pink Floyd in their rock-opera 'The Wall' and in the Alan Parker film version capture the insensitivity and cruelty that many experienced. Because we do not relate very well with ourselves many others are hurt in relationships. Words left unsaid, harsh words expressed, communicate rejection and generate lack of acceptance in the other. So often relationships fail because we do not communicate very well. People who feel unwanted can fill in the gaps I have left with their own stories. My list is not exhaustive.

How does loneliness and lack of self-acceptance feel? Music, art, film often help us find expression. Trying to put words on the experience of aloneness and lostness often fail and leave us empty. Georges Bernanos (+1948) was a French writer who could express the loneliness of his heroes and heroines better than any I know. In his 1937 work "Nouvelle Histoire de Mouchette" he paints a tragic picture of Mouchette (whose name means literally "little fly"). For Bernanos modern life is men in anguish. Anguish has taken the place of faith. All that is seen is frenzied activity, but this is the form anguish takes. This is the world Mouchette lives in and with her all of us. Bernanos drew on St. Thérèse of Lisieux and her "love", her "universal love". Mouchette is the anti-type of Thérèse. Her family is abusive, she is abused and bullied and rejected in school. This overcomes her and she takes her life. Bernanos refused to call her death suicide, saying she reached out for the hand of comfort and reassurance that was never extended. Reading Mouchette focusses on Thérèse and her love for all the broken. Her love was to be the hand that reached other "Mouchettes" of our world. In the "Diary of a Country Priest" the lonely curé says he is a "prisoner of the Holy Agony" (Diary of a Country Priest, p. 222). He is able to extend to others the joy he does not feel.

Robert Bresson (+1999) was a famous film director. In his early films he was an interpreter of Bernanos. Martin Scorcese admired Bresson and remarked at how he would have loved to make as bleak a scene as Bresson had in his earlier films. In 1967 he made a film based on "Nouvelle Histoire de Mouchette" called simply "Mouchette". At the end of the film when Mouchette takes her life one hears the strings of Monteverdi's "Magnificat". By this device he hoped to show Mouchette is held in the arms of grace. Bresson says that Mouchette is to be found everywhere – in prisons, concentration camps, torture camps and in all situations where the vulnerable are crushed and abused.[1] Bernanos in his work "Un Mauvais Rêve (1950) (An Evil Dream) speaks of the 'great hatred' that haunts humanity:

> "When nervous frenzy passes a certain point and dread (épouvante) itself seems to have found its balance in a

---

[1] See my Thérèse and the Little Way of Love and Healing (Athlone: 2013).

frightful immobility, then the strongest instinct of which a living being is capable – self-defense – appears in effect to have been abolished. For the poor wretch caught in the throes of this condition, it is then a question no longer of escaping from his pain and anguish but of exhausting it. At its climax, every form of madness succeeds in baring the bottommost foundation of man's soul – that secret self-hatred that is the deepest part of his life, and probably of every life."

(Un Mauvais Rêve, p. 237f)

In the Nouvelle Histoire de Mouchette this 'fear' is the basis for all the characters seeking pleasure, but never finding it. In the Diary of a Country Priest he writes:

"There is in man a secret, incomprehensible hatred, not only of his fellowmen, but of himself. We can give this mysterious feeling whatever origin or explanation we want, but we must give it one. As far as we Christians are concerned, we believe that this hatred reflects another hatred, a thousand times more profound and lucid: the hatred of the ineffable spirit who was the most resplendent of all the luminaries of the abyss and who will never forgive us his cataclysmic fall. Outside the hypothesis of an original sin, that is, of an intrinsic contradiction within our nature, the notion of man does become quite clear, only it is no longer the notion of man. When this occurs, man has gone straight through the definition of man, like a handful of sand running between his fingers."

(Diary, p. 29)

We live in a land "East of Eden" and we feel the loss of this Paradise. Many events and more importantly people teach us of our inadequacies. Advertising plays on our fears. Deep down we find it difficult to love ourselves. To truly love and accept oneself is truly the grace of graces. Abuse and rejection plunge us deeper and deeper into this world of self-loathing.

Psalm 88 is a psalm that expresses deep loneliness. It is one of the most sombre pieces of writing in the Old Testament and expresses in faith before God what it means to feel the loss of his Presence. Before the silence of God the psalmist looks at his pain and pours out his complaint to God. He is like 'Antigone' of Greek tragedy who says goodbye to the light.

The psalm begins with an appeal to God:

> "Yahweh, God of my salvation,
> when I cry out in the night,
> May my prayer reach your presence.
> hear my cry for help."   (Ps 88:1-2)

He comes to cry to God but now God is silent. Jesus' prison would have been just a hole in the ground (the site is marked by San Pietro in Gallicantu in Jerusalem). As the stone was rolled back he found himself surrounded by darkness and loneliness. He feels the lack of the Presence of the Father who is silent.

Ps 55 helps us appreciate the loneliness of Ps 88:

> "My heart is in anguish within me,
> the terrors of death have fallen upon me.
> Fear and trembling come upon me,
> and horror overwhelms me."   (Ps 55:4-5)

Ps 88 finishes thus:

> "They surround me all the day like a flood,
> they assail me all together,
> Friend and neighbour you have taken away:
> my one companion is darkness.   (Ps 88:17-18)

The psalmist feels the loss of God and the loss of all his friends. He has no more supports. All that is left to him is darkness.

The Lonely City:

You can be lonely anywhere, but there is a particular flavour to the loneliness that comes from living in a city, surrounded by millions of people. One might think this state was antithetical to urban living, to the massed presence of other human beings, and yet mere physical proximity is not enough to dispel a sense of internal isolation. It's possible – easy, even – to feel desolate and unfrequented in oneself while living cheek by jowl with others. Cities can be lonely places, and in admitting this we see that loneliness doesn't necessarily require physical solitude, but rather an absence or paucity of connection, closeness, kinship: an inability, for one reason or another, to find as much intimacy as is desired. Unhappy, as the dictionary has it, as a result of being without the companionship of others. Hardly any wonder, then, that it can reach its apotheosis in a crowd.

> Loneliness is difficult to confess, difficult too to categorise. Like depression, a state with which it often intersects, it can run deep in the fabric of a person, as much a part of one's being as laughing easily or having red hair. Then again, it can be transient, lapping in and out in reaction to external circumstance, like the loneliness that follows on the heels of a bereavement, break-up or change in social circles.
>
> (Olivia Laing, The Lonely City, p. 3f)

Olivia Laing[2] experienced the break-up of a relationship and left her native England to live in New York. This was a time for her of loneliness and loss. Yet in her loneliness she found that this pit could "drive one to consider the larger questions of what it is to be alive". She questioned whether technology helped us deal with loneliness or were we just trapped behind big screens. Laing was partly inspired by the loneliness described by Virginia Woolf in her diaries and how she used this loneliness to create a solitude out of which was born her creativity. Laing chooses four artists as her companions, companions who knew loneliness from the inside yet turned their pain into creativity. She chose Edward Hopper, Andy Warhol, Henry Darger and Daniel Wojnarowicz.

[2] O. Laing, The Lonely City: Adventures in the Art of Being Alone (Edinburgh: 2016).

She was not initially attracted to Andy Warhol (+1987) until she was lonely. At the time of her loneliness she found it difficult to communicate – she thought of dumbness as being a way of avoiding hurt and contact with the other.

> "Dumbness in this context might be a way of evading hurt, dodging the pain of failed communication by refusing to participate in it at all. That's how I explained my growing silence, anyway; as an aversion akin to someone wishing to avoid a repeated electric shock.
> If anyone would have understood this dilemma, it was Andy Warhol, an artist I'd always dismissed until I became lonely myself. I'd seen the screen-printed cows and Chairman Maos a thousand times, and I thought they were vacuous and empty, disregarding them as we often do with things we've looked at but failed properly to see. My fascination with Warhol did not begin until after I'd moved to New York, when I happened upon a couple of his television interviews one day on YouTube and was struck by how hard he seemed to be struggling with the demands of speech."
>
> (Lonely City, p. 50)

She learned that Warhol rarely left the house without an array of cameras and tape-recorders, so that he had a barrier against human contact. Yet when she looked again at his art she could feel the presence of the artist behind the reproductions. He creates a closeness and at the same time a distance between people. Loneliness is barren and destructive yet in the hands of an artist such as Warhol and the others, a creative solitude is made out of the loneliness and new forms of expression and art are born. Even in the darkness a light, a dim light, shines, and this light can grow. When Laing looked at Virginia Woolf's diary writings on loneliness and creativity, she said "loneliness might be taking you towards an otherwise unreachable experience of reality" (p. 4).

> "The janitor and outsider artist Henry Darger inhabited the opposite extreme. He lived alone in a boarding house in the city of Chicago, creating in a near-total void of

companionship or audience a fictional universe populated by wonderful and frightening beings. When he gave up his room unwillingly at the age of seventy to die in a Catholic mission home, it was found to be stuffed with hundreds of exquisite and disturbing paintings, work he'd apparently never shown to another human being. Darger's life illuminates the social forces that drive isolation – and the way the imagination can work to resist it."

(Lonely City, p. 6)

This introduces us to the figure of Henry Darger (+1973). She speaks of Edward Hopper (+1967) and his images of solitary men and women glimpsed behind glass in deserted cafes, offices and hotel lobbies remain the signature images of isolation in the big cities. David Wojnarowicz's (+1992) courageous body of work did more than anything to release Laing from the burden of feeling that in her solitude she was shamefully alone. In the epigraph of her book she quotes St. Paul: "and every one members of one another". Those who have experienced loneliness and developed an artistic expression of it are a gift to all of us.

The Smiths were a north of England rock band formed in Manchester in 1982. Their music was moody and melancholic. Steven Patrick Morrissey (professionally known as Morrissey) was the lead singer with the Smiths and was a song-writer and author. The Smiths were English but had roots in Ireland. Morrissey experienced anti-Irish sentiment as a young man. This sense of dislocation and not quite belonging formed their music. When Morrissey and the Smiths played Galway, Ireland, they would say it was like a homecoming. Morrissey was also disturbed by such events as the Moors murders. Yet in one of their songs we hear the lines: "There is a light that never goes out". The song begins:

"Take me out tonight
Where there's music and there's people
And they're young and alive
Driving in your car
I never want to go home

Because I haven't got one
Anymore."

We hear the sense of loneliness and dislocation. He says of home that "… it's their home and I'm welcome no more". Yet the song ends with the line "There is a light and it never goes out" and this is repeated. In the darkness there is always that glimmer of light. In 2004, BBC Radio 4 asks listeners to tell them which records made them want to cry, to shout out and feel better. This song was one of the songs chosen by the listeners.

A Season in Hell

Arthur Rimbaud (real name Jean Nicolas Arthur Rimbaud, 1854 – 1891) was a French poet who had a profound influence on the world of art after his death. He was a child prodigy but he stopped working in poetry completely at the age of 21. He began to travel and did not again write poetry. He was known in his youth as a libertine and a restless soul. He had a tempestuous love affair with the poet Paul Verlaine (+1896). He was a symbolist poet. In 1873 in the Hotel Liège in Brussels, Rimbaud and Verlaine took refuge in heavy drinking. Later they had an argument and Verlaine shot Rimbaud. He survived but the affair was over. In the hotel today tourists can visit the spot where Verlaine tried to kill Rimbaud. One of his favourite sayings was "Je est un autre!" – translated literally it says "I is the other". The grammar is all out of kilter but the sentiment can be felt. It is only in relation to others that I become myself. Rimbaud said:

"The idea is to reach the unknown by the derangement of
all the senses. It involves enormous suffering but one must
be strong and be a born poet."
(Letter to Georges Izambard, 13 May 1871).

And again he compares himself to a "seer", on who sees:

"I say that one must be a seer. The poet makes himself a
seer by a long, prodigious, and rational disordering of all

the senses. Every form of love, of suffering, of madness; he searches himself, he consumes all the poisons in him, and keeps only their quintessences. This is an unspeakable torture during which he needs all his faith..."

(Letter to Paul Demeny, 15 May 1871,
retrieved on May 12th 2011).

Jim Morrison of the Doors was influenced by Rimbaud. The "derangement of all the senses" is a line used by Jim Morrison (played by Val Kilmer) in the 1991 film 'The Doors' (directed by Oliver Stone). Rimbaud's poetry was a cry for salvation, a cry for the one who would meet him and give him life and heal his wounds. This is the other (l'autre) that Rimbaud sought. In the music of people like Led Zeppelin, The Rolling Stones and Pink Floyd there is an expression, especially in the guitar work of Keith Richards, Jimmy Page and David Gilmour, of this 'derangement of the senses' and a reaching out for healing, for the other to meet us, and love us. Some zealots tried to tell us that this was demonic. If we played our records backwards we would hear strange things. However, records at that time could only be played forward. Many kids ruined their expensive Led Zeppelin LPs by trying to push the needle backwards. Many lonely people (myself included) have found solace in listening to these musicians. Music can express what words cannot – the profound 'derangement of the senses' expresses the unknown. Rimbaud also influenced Bob Dylan. In a scene from the film "I'm Not There" (2007) a young Bob Dylan is portrayed identifying himself as Arthur Rimbaud.

"A Season in Hell" (in French: Une Saison en Enfer) is an extensive prose poem which Rimbaud wrote in 1873. The first copies were panned by the critics. It was also at the time of Rimbaud's tempestuous shooting by Verlaine. The public were not sympathetic to Rimbaud. He cancelled all publication of his work and never wrote again. Rimbaud feels he is in Hell in the poem and in need of someone's hand to lead him through. He opens the poem and introduces the work as "pages from the diary of a damned soul". The Night of Hell ("Nuit de l'Enfer) highlights the moments of the narrator's death and entry into Hell. He describes the Night in the following words:

"I have just swallowed a terrific mouthful of poison. - Blessed, blessed, blessed the advice I was given! - My guts are on fire. The power of the poison twists my arms and legs, cripples me, drives me to the ground. I die of thirst, I suffocate, I cannot cry. This is Hell, eternal torment! See how the flames rise! I burn as I ought to…"

Later he says:

"But I am still alive! - Suppose damnation is eternal! A man who wants to mutilate himself is certainly damned, isn't he? I believe I am in Hell, therefore I am. This is the catechism at work."

In his description of Hell Rimbaud pens all his fears and expresses his loneliness. This ironically is his release from Hell. He finds his salvation in the beauty of poetry. He has reached out to find the other (l'autre). At the end of the poem he is released from Hell and lives again. In reading the poem and contemplating the mystery he enables us to confront our loneliness and fears and one day come to a new light. This is the journey of this book. After Rimbaud's death his work was rediscovered and republished. Rimbaud influenced artists, writers and musicians as we have seen. He influenced the art movement known as Dada and Surrealism. He influenced people like André Breton, Pablo Picasso and Vladimir Nabokov. Rimbaud's life has been portrayed in several films. One such film is Nelo Risi's 'Una Stagione all'Inferno' (1971) starring Terence Stamp as Rimbaud and Jean-Claud Brialy as Paul Verlaine. Rimbaud is mentioned in the film 'Eddie and the Cruisers' (1983). In the storyline the groups's second album was entitled 'A Season in Hell'. In 1995 Polish filmmaker Agnieszka Holland directed 'Total Eclipse' which starred Leonardo DiCaprio as Rimbaud. In the film 'Pollock' (2000), Lee Krasner (played by Marcia Gay Harden) reads a quote from "A Season in Hell" written on the wall of her studio, when she first receives a visit from Jackson Pollock (played by Ed Harris):

"To whom shall I hire myself out?
What beast must I adore?

What holy image is attacked?
What hearts must I break?
What lie must I maintain? In what blood tread?"

Rimbaud's "Season in Hell" gave life to many.

Art is to Console Those Broken by Life (Van Gogh)

Vincent Van Gogh was born in Groot-Zundert, Holland, on March 30, 1853. He was the son of a pastor, brought up in a religious and cultural environment. He was highly emotional, lacked self-confidence and struggled with his identity and with direction. Like Warhol he also found it hard to communicate and would feel locked up inside of himself. He believed that his true calling was to preach the Gospel. In the end he found his calling in Art. He confided to his brother Theo that the world needed a new teaching of religion. Between 1860 and 1880 Van Gogh had experienced two unsuitable and unhappy romances, and had worked unsuccessfully as a clerk in a bookstore, an art salesman, and a preacher in the Borinage (a dreary mining district in Belgium) where he was dismissed for overzealousness.

He remained in Belgium to study Art, determined to bring healing by creating beauty. Just as Jesus used the ordinary materials of earth to teach of God and his love in parables, so Vincent helped to create the same effect by showing the beauty that lies in the world. All beauty for Vincent is a reflection of the Divine. In his early period in Belgium his work was grim, however. His best work from that period was "The Potato Eaters" (1885). In Belgium he went on to discover the works of Rubens and purchased many Japanese prints.

He had a close relationship with his brother Theo. Over the years they wrote to each other very often. After Belgium, Vincent lived with Theo in Paris and there he discovered the works of Gauguin and the Impressionists. In 1888 Van Gogh went to Arles and helped to form a community of painters. However Gauguin was the only one who came and their time together ended in acrimony, ending with the famous cutting off by Vincent of part of his ear. Both Gauguin and Van Gogh refused to give too much information on this strange event and the whole affair is still a mystery. During this time Van Gogh's mental health continued to suffer and he spent time in an asylum in Saint-Rémy. In May 1890 he seemed to be a little better. He went to Auvers-sur-Oise under the watchful eye of Dr. Gachet. Two months later he died from what is believed to have been a self-inflicted wound, though questions still remain.[3] During his life he only sold one painting. Yet it is ironic that at the time of his death critics were beginning to notice his work. However, during Vincent's life he lived in poverty, and was malnourished and overworked. The money he had was supplied by Theo and was used principally for his art supplies, coffee and cigarettes. Van Gogh is for me what the other artists are for Olivia Laing (The Lonely City). Van Gogh claimed there in nothing more artistic in life than to love people. He would pour that love into his paintings, but by putting his heart and soul into his work he lost his mental health. He would speak to Theo of having a great fire in his heart, but no-one would care to warm themselves by that fire. Passers-by would only see a wisp of smoke. He also believed that there was a divine spark in everyone and he hoped his work would set that spark free in people who came to see his work.

Vincent was filled with a reverence for something greater than himself. He looked to the night sky as a source of faith and hope. The year before Vincent was born a brother, also named Vincent, was born and died. His mother was in grief when the new boy, also called Vincent, was born and he felt this placed a distance between her and him. This led Vincent to feeling inferior and hypersensitive. This sensitivity continued to undermine his self-confidence and contributed to recurring bouts of deep sadness that in later years turned to depression. At the root of Vincent's sorrow was a yearning for love, acceptance and affirmation. His low self-esteem was aggravated by the high expectations his father had for him. His father hoped Vincent would follow him into the ministry but was disappointed when Vincent turned his mind towards art. Vincent and his father had arguments about the realist novels Vincent read, with Vincent trying unsuccessfully to convince his father

[3] see Stephen Naifeh and Gregory White Smith, Van Gogh: The Life (New York: 2011).

that the Gospel message was as clearly expressed in contemporary novels as it was in the Bible. Pastor Van Gogh felt his son berated his faith and life work.

After the death of his father and before leaving the parsonage, Vincent painted one of his most personally expressive paintings "Still Life with Bible" (1885). The painting shows an old Bible resting on a table, opened to the passage of the "Suffering Servant" in the book of Isaiah. Beside the book is a worn-out copy of the novel "La Joie de Vivre" (The Joy of Living) by Emile Zola. Zola's introduction to this novel gives a sense of the powerful story:

> "She [Pauline Quenu, the servant girl] would remain unmarried in order to be able to work for universal deliverance. And she was, indeed, the incarnation of renunciation, of love for others and kindly charity for erring humanity. She had stripped herself of everything, but happiness rang out in her clear laugh."

For Vincent these stories do not diminish the Bible, but show us the meaning of the Bible story for today. Vincent was influenced at this stage by Franz Hals and Delacroix's theory of colour. Vincent succeeded in blending the holy and timeless scripture into the meaning of life, personal loss and eternal truths that connected the present with the past and future. The hymn of the Suffering Servant from Isaiah 53 summoned up for Vincent the Jesus with whom he so identified. Vincent knew grief, depression and as he became more eccentric he experienced more and more rejection. He had given a visual voice to his sorrow, his regret, his longing for forgiveness. It was a plea for a spiritual reconciliation with his father. The extinguished candle next to the Bible signifies death, yet the subtle complementary colours of blue and orange reveal life. This life could be seen in works like Zola and ultimately in the art of Van Gogh.

Van Gogh made use of the olive tree as a visual emblem of Christ. Gethsemane, in Hebrew, refers to an olive press. We see his attitude to the propriety of painting biblical subjects in a letter to Theo:

"However, now is not the moment to ask me to admire our friend Gauguin's composition, and our friend Bernard has probably never seen an olive tree. Now he is avoiding getting the least idea of the possible, or of the reality of things, and that is not the way to synthesise – no, I have never taken any stock in their biblical interpretations.

I said that Rembrandt and Delacroix had done this admirably, that I liked it even better than the primitives... If I stay here, I shall not try to paint "Christ in the Garden of Olives", but the glowing of the olives as you still see it, giving nevertheless the exact proportions of the human figure in it, perhaps that would make people think."

(Edge of Eternity, p. 151)

Émil Bernard (+1941) was a painter friend of Van Gogh. He was a Catholic and a mystic who influenced Van Gogh in both art and religious experience. Van Gogh did not agree however with Bernard's depictions of biblical subjects. He wrote to Bernard:

"...One can try to give an impression of anguish without aiming straight at the historic Garden of Gethsemane; ...it is not necessary to portray the characters of the Sermon on the Mount in order to produce a consoling and gentle motif. Oh! undoubtedly it is wise and proper to be moved by the Bible, but modern reality has got such a hold on us that, even when we attempt to reconstruct the ancient days in our thoughts abstractly, the minor events of our lives tear us away from our meditations, and our own adventures thrust us back into our personal sensations – joy, boredom, suffering, anger, or a smile.

The Bible! The Bible! Miller, having been brought up on it from infancy, did nothing but read that book! And yet he never, or hardly ever, painted Biblical pictures. Corot has done a "Mount of Olives", with Christ and the evening star, sublime; in his works one feels Homer, Aeschylus, Sophocles, as well as the Gospel sometimes, yet how discreet it is, and how much all possible modern sensations, common to us all, predominate.

...Being able to divide a canvas into great planes which intermingle, to find lines, forms which make contrasts, that is technique, tricks if you like, cuisine, but it is a sign all the same that you are studying your handicraft more deeply, and that is a good thing."

(Edge of Eternity, p. 152)

At St. Rémy he also painted iconographic religious subjects, The Pietà, The Raising of Lazarus, and the Good Samaritan. He chose to rework these subjects, which are images of sorrow and deliverance, death and resurrection. By replacing the face of Christ in the Pietà, as well as Lazarus in The Raising of Lazarus, with his own face, Van Gogh deliberately displayed his identification with both the pain and regeneration of the subjects.

Divine Love is revealed in beauty. Beauty is seen in a tangible, visible form. Van Gogh infuses his work with love and the beholder is drawn into this love, this acceptance. In the same way Jesus reveals the love of God and in contemplating him one is drawn into his love and shares the love he has with the Father. The Spirit is the medium of this love. The result is an encounter between my "I" and the Thou of God. God's love is a love that searches for our hearts and calls us to share in God's love, by the power of the Holy Spirit. The disfigured face of the suffering Jesus seems to be the opposite of beauty. Yet in contemplation we are led to the infinite love of Jesus for the broken and we come to know his inner beauty. Jesus died not write but those who followed wrote words of faith that we now call the New Testament. In contemplating these we come to Jesus and are transformed in love by the Holy Spirit.[4] Ultimately it is love that leads us out of loneliness.

God's name for us is beautiful. He sees the inner goodness we can become in the light of his love by the power of the Holy Spirit. In Rev

---

[4] For the use of beauty in theology see Hans Urs Von Balthasar, Love Alone is Credible (San Francisco: 2004) and The Glory of the Lord: Seeing the Form, vol 1, trans. Erasmo Leiva-Merikakis (San Francisco: 1982).

2:17 the one who overcomes and finds peace in God is given a special white stone with a name known only to God and the one who receives the stone. This signifies the true person one is called to become. St. John of the Cross in his commentary on the Canticle says:

"Let us go forth to behold ourselves in your beauty,

This means: Let us so act that by means of this loving activity we may attain to the vision of ourselves in your beauty in eternal life. That is: That I be so transformed in your beauty that we may be alike in beauty, and both behold ourselves in your beauty, possessing then your very beauty; this, in such a way that each looking at the other may see in the other their own beauty, since both are your beauty alone, I being absorbed in your beauty; hence, I shall see you in your beauty, and you will see me in your beauty, and I shall see myself in you in your beauty, and you will see yourself in me in your beauty; that I may resemble you in your beauty, and you resemble me in your beauty, and my beauty be your beauty and your beauty be my beauty; wherefore I shall be you in your beauty, and you will be me in your beauty, because your very beauty will be my beauty; and thus we shall behold each other in your beauty."

(C 31:5)

Chapter 2

We Would Like to See Jesus (Jn 12:21)

In the midst of loneliness we would like to meet Jesus as the Greeks who spoke to Philip wanted to meet him (Jn 12:21). It is through the example of eyewitnesses that we get to know Jesus. One of the strangest eyewitnesses was Paul of Tarsus. I say he was 'strange' because he did not meet Jesus during his lifetime. He met Jesus the resurrected Jesus and this turned his life around.

Paul does not tell us where he was born but his name Paulos, would connect him with a Roman town. He boasted of his Jewish background and he traced his background to the tribe of Benjamin (Rom 1:1; Phil 3:5; 2 Cor 11:22). He was an Israelite, "a Hebrew born of Hebrews… as to the law a Pharisee (Phil 3:5). He was extremely zealous for the traditions of his fathers and one who excelled his peers in Judaism (Gal 1:14).

In the Acts of the Apostles Luke presents Paul as a jew born in Tarsus (Acts 22:3; 21:39), as having a sister (23:16) and as a Roman citizen from birth (Acts 22:25-29, 16:37; 23:27). In Pompey's reorganisation of Asia Minor in 66 BC Tarsus became the capital of the province of Cilicia. Tarsus was a well known centre of culture, philosophy and education (Strabo, Geogr).

In the Acts we hear Paul boast of being brought up in Jerusalem and educated at the feet of Gamaliel (Acts 22:3). Gamaliel was active in Jerusalem from ca 20-50 AD.[1] According to Joachim Jeremias, Paul at the time of his conversion was a recognised teacher with the right to make legal decisions.[2] This authority would be seen in his right to go to Damascus to arrest Christians (Acts 9:1-2; 22:4-5; 26:12).

---

[1] W.C. van Unnik, Tarsus or Jerusalem: The City of Paul's Youth (London: 1962).

[2] J. Jeremias, ZNW 25 (1926), p. 310-312, ZNW 28 (1929), p. 321-323.

In the Acts of the Apostles we are introduced to the figure of Paul/Saul at the murder of Stephen:

> But Stephen, filled with the Holy Spirit, gazed into heaven and saw the glory of God, and Jesus standing at God's right hand. 'Look! I can see heaven thrown open,' he said, 'and the Son of man standing at the right hand of God.' All the members of the council shouted out and stopped their ears with their hands; then they made a concerted rush at him, thrust him out of the city and stoned him. The witnesses put down their clothes at the feet of a young man called Saul. As they were stoning him, Stephen said in invocation, 'Lord Jesus, receive my spirit.' Then he knelt down and said aloud, 'Lord, do not hold this sin against them.' And with these words he fell asleep.
> Saul approved of the killing.
> That day a bitter persecution started against the church in Jerusalem, and everyone except the apostles scattered to the country districts of Judaea and Samaria.
> There were some devout people, however, who buried Stephen and made great mourning for him.
> Saul then began doing great harm to the church; he went from house to house arresting both men and women and sending them to prison.
>
> (Acts 7:55-8:3)

Stoning outside the city (Lev 24:14, Num 15:35-36, m Sanh 6:1) pertains to the prophet murder traditions received by Luke (see Lk 4:29; 13:34; 20:15). Paul is present and consents. The Christian Hellenists were expelled from Jerusalem and Paul was actively involved in their persecution.

Paul's "Conversion":

Luke recounts Paul's Damascus experience three times in the book of the Acts of the Apostles, the first time in 9:3-19 and twice in speeches, one before a crowd in Jerusalem (22:6-16) and before Festus and King Agrippa (26:12-18). Paul regarded his experience near Damascus as life-changing. This meeting with the risen Jesus was one he would never forget. When his apostolate was questioned he would respond: "Am I not an apostle? Have I not seen Jesus our Lord" (1 Cor 9:1, cf 15:8). As a result of that revelation of Jesus Christ (Gal 1:12), he became a servant of Jesus Christ (Gal 1:10). In Acts 19:3-19 we read:

The conversion of Saul
Meanwhile Saul was still breathing threats to slaughter the Lord's disciples. He went to the high priest and asked for letters addressed to the synagogues in Damascus, that would authorise him to arrest and take to Jerusalem any followers of the Way, men or women, that he might find.
It happened that while he was travelling to Damascus and approaching the city, suddenly a light from heaven shone all round him. He fell to the ground, and then he heard a voice saying, 'Saul, Saul, why are you persecuting me?' 'Who are you, Lord?' he asked, and the answer came, 'I am Jesus, whom you are persecuting. Get up and go into the city, and you will be told what you are to do.' The men travelling with Saul stood there speechless, for though they heard the voice they could see no one. Saul got up from the ground, but when he opened his eyes he could see nothing at all, and they had to lead him into Damascus by the hand. For three days he was without his sight and took neither food nor drink.
There was a disciple in Damascus called Ananias, and he had a vision in which the Lord said to him, 'Ananias!' When he replied, 'Here I am, Lord,' the Lord said, 'Get up and go to Straight Street and ask at the house of Judas for someone called Saul, who comes from Tarsus. At this moment he is praying, and has seen a man called Ananias coming in and laying hands on him to give him back his sight.'
But in response, Ananias said, 'Lord, I have heard from many people about this man and all the harm he has been doing to your holy people in Jerusalem. He has come here with a warrant from the chief priests to arrest everybody who

invokes your name.' The Lord replied, 'Go, for this man is my chosen instrument to bring my name before gentiles and kings and before the people of Israel; I myself will show him how much he must suffer for my name.' Then Ananias went. He entered the house, and laid his hands on Saul and said, 'Brother Saul, I have been sent by the Lord Jesus, who appeared to you on your way here, so that you may recover your sight and be filled with the Holy Spirit.' It was as though scales fell away from his eyes and immediately he was able to see again. So he got up and was baptised, and after taking some food he regained his strength.

Saul is blinded by the light. He hears a voice asking him "why do you persecute me?" In his disciples the Lord is persecuted. This is the answer Paul/Saul gets to his question. He has come to meet the resurrected Jesus. The dreaded persecutor is now immobilised and is led to Damascus. Ananias is commissioned to heal Saul, but he is afraid of him because of his reputation. To reassure Ananias the risen one points out Saul is his "chosen one". In the name of Jesus who appeared to Saul, Ananias goes and prays for Saul who recovers. He is now filled with the Holy Spirit.

Saul becomes a zealous preacher to the people he once persecuted. Luke, with a touch of humour, says after Saul was sent home to take a break: "The churches throughout Judaea, Galilee and Samaria were now left in peace" (Acts 9:31).

In the early part of the 20th century, under the influence of Reinach, it was proposed that the early Christians had conformed the story of Jesus to pagan legends and mystery cults surrounding the dying and rising gods (Attis, Adonis, Osiris, Dionysius).[3]

Wolfhart Pannenberg (1928-2014) points us towards the history of the event. Paul believed he had seen the risen Lord (Gal 1:12,16) and that many others had seen Jesus (1 Cor 15:5-8). Pannenberg says that the

---

[3] R.E. Brown, The Resurrection of Jesus in Aspects of New Testament Thought, NJBC, p. 1374f.

resurrection is not the simple resuscitation of a corpse. Paul insists that what died was perishable, weak and mortal but what rises is imperishable, glorious and immortal (15:42-43; 32-34). In short "it is sown in a physical body; it is raised as a spiritual body (1 Cor 15:44). There is a transformation, but it is Jesus who is transformed. The crucified one is now alive and is immortal. He lives with God forever. Pannenberg writes:

> "Something happened in which the disciples in these appearances were confronted with a reality which also in our language cannot be expressed in any other way than the symbolic and metaphorical expression of the hope beyond death, the resurrection from the dead. Please understand me correctly: Only the name we give to the event is symbolic, metaphorical, but not the reality of the event itself. The latter is so absolutely unique that we have no other name for this than the metaphorical expression of the apocalyptic expectation. In this sense, the resurrection of Jesus is an historical event, an event that really happened at that time."[4]

The event of Jesus' resurrection is something out of our view of normality. Many of the attempts to understand the mystery try to reduce it to something that seems "reasonable". Pannenberg lives more with the mystery and the unpacking of the meaning of the resurrection appearances is something that we continue to wrestle with. The truth in the end is that Jesus overcame death and lives now at the right hand of God. He is alive today. This is what Paul found out and this turned his worldview around. In this sense we speak of his "conversion".

Prayer in Paul

Praying is one of the most human things we can do. Yet we tie ourselves in many questions and prefer to discuss than to pray. Yet Paul

---

[4] W. Pannenberg, Did Jesus Really Rise from the Dead? Dialog 4 (1965) 125-135 at p. 135. See also his Jesus – God and Man (Phil: 1968).

demonstrates a deep prayer-ful existence. There are two examples of blessings directed to God for experiences Paul received.[5] The two blessing formulae are found in 2 Cor 1:3-11 and Eph 1:3-14. Paul praises the "God and Father of our Lord Jesus Christ..." (2 Cor 1:3; Eph 1:3). He mentions in particular a grave situation where he had almost given up hope (2 Cor 1:8-11). In Ephesians he praises God for the way he has chosen and guided him as an apostle (Eph 1:4-14). Blessings form part and parcel of the life of the people of the Old and New Testament (e.g. Gen 9; Ex 18:10; Lk 1:68-79; 1 Pt 1:3-9; 1 QM 18:6-7; 1 QM 11:15) and there is a long treatment of the berakhot (blessings in the Mishnah etc.). In the letter to Titus Paul says: "To Titus, true child of mine in the faith we share. Grace and peace from God the Father and from Jesus Christ our saviour." (Titus 1:4).

Paul thanks God and uses little formulae of thanksgiving (with the use of the verb eucharistein [see 1 Th 2:13; 2 Th 2:13] and it is used with the word charis [grace] in 1 Cor 15:15; 2 Cor 2:14; 8:16; 9:15; Rom 6:17; 7:25; 2 Tim 1:3). At Qumran this prayer was discovered (1 QH): "Thank you Adonai (Lord)... and source of all power..." (1 QH 1:1). Qumran is an area in the desert where a Jewish sect called the Essenes lived. They lived about the time of Jesus. It was founded about 130 B.C. In 1947 a number of scrolls were found. They contain the books of the Bible, commentaries (pesher) on the texts and the prayers of the community, like the above.

Central to the life of prayer is God's empowering presence in the Holy Spirit. In Romans Paul says: "...the Spirit too comes to help us in our weakness, for when we do not know how to pray properly, then the Spirit personally makes our petition for us in groans that cannot be put into words and he who can see into our hearts knows what the Spirit means because the prayers that the Spirit makes for God's holy people are always in accordance with the mind of God." (Rom 8:26f). It is the Spirit who inspires our prayer and completes it. The one who sees into our hearts is God the Father. It is the same Spirit who calls out to the

---

[5] N.T. Wright in his work, Paul and the Faithfulness of God (London: 2013) argues that all the letters (Pauline and Deutero-Pauline) be attributed to Paul. I follow him.

Father as "Abba: Father" (see Rom 8:15; Gal 4:6-7). 'Abba' is the name Jesus gave to his Father when he prayed in agony in Gethsemane (Mk 14:36). It speaks of the intimacy of Father and child; we are God's children and beloved of him. We have "received the Spirit of adoption, enabling us to cry out, "Abba, Father". The Spirit himself joins himself with our spirit to bear witness that we are children of God." (Rom 8:15f).

To use an image from St. John, "The wind blows where it pleases, you hear its sound, but you cannot tell where it comes from or where it is going. So it is with everyone who is born of the Spirit" (Jn 3:8). With those who pray in the Spirit they find themselves like birds of the air moved by the wind. The air is the environment in which they live and move. Those who pray find themselves in the space of the Spirit[6] and it is in him that we and our prayer lives and moves and has its being. We say we pray "in the Spirit". For Paul, Jesus is revealed as the Son of God by the power of the Holy Spirit. The presence of the resurrected Jesus is made possible by the action of the Holy Spirit. This same Spirit transformed Saul into Paul. In this Spirit Paul urges his listeners to "pray constantly" (1 Thess 5:17) and in the letter to the Ephesians we read: "In all your prayer and entreaty keep praying in the Sprit on every possible occasion. Never get tired of staying awake to pray for all God's holy people" (Eph 6:18). Paul received the Gospel by the power of the Holy Spirit (Rom 1:9) and he asks the Ephesians to pray for him (Eph 6:19) that he might pass this Gospel on with the courage he needs from the Holy Spirit. The love of God has been poured into his heart by the Holy Spirit (Rom 5:5) and he wishes to bring others into that love. As we saw when he cannot find the words to pray as he ought the Spirit prays in him (Rom 8:26f).

We see that Paul's theology is a theology that comes from his life of prayer. He reflects on his life with God and Jesus in the power of the Holy Spirit. Paul saw the risen Jesus. His reflections lead us to an understanding of God revealed in Jesus. Paul's vision was not for

[6] M. Chiolerio, Lo Spirito Santo nella Preghiera, in Enciclopedia della Preghiera (Rome: 2007) p. 132ff.

himself only. It was for us. Paul's experience confronts us with the reality of the risen Jesus and our call to new life in him by the power of the Holy Spirit. In the Acts of the Apostles the risen Lord says to Ananias, "Go, for this man is my chosen instrument to bring my name before the gentiles and kings and before the people of Israel." (Acts 9:15).

St. John of the Cross describes the Holy Spirit as the "Living Flame of Love", the love that unites Father and Son.[7] The First Stanza reads:

> "O living flame of love
> That tenderly wounds my soul
> In its deepest center! Since
> Now you are not oppressive,
> Now consummate! if it be your will:
> Tear through the veil of this sweet encounter!"

By the power of the Holy Spirit the soul lives in this profound union of Father and Son. The Holy Spirit is the medium of love in which the soul lives and is called by John "O living flame of love." The flame of love is the "Spirit of the Bridegroom, who is the Holy Spirit. The soul feels him within itself not only as a fire that has consumed and transformed it but as a fire that burns and flares within it... and that flame, every time it flares up, bathes the soul in glory and refreshes it with the quality of divine life." (Living Flame, 1:3). The Spirit inspires acts of love which are pure without an admixture of selfishness. "These acts of love are most precious; one of them is more meritorious and valuable than all the deeds a person may have performed in the whole of life without this transformation..." (Living Flame, 1:3)

He goes on to use the image of a log of wood being transformed in the fire to show how we are transformed in love by the Holy Spirit. He says: "We can compare the soul in its ordinary condition in this state of transformation of love to the log of wood that is ever immersed in fire,

---

[7] See The Living Flame of Love in Collected Works of St. John of the Cross (Washington: 1991) translated by Kieran Kavanagh, O.C.D. and Otilio Rodriguez, O.C.D.

and the acts of this soul to the flame that blazes up from the fire of love. The more intense the fire of union, the more vehemently does this fire burst into flames." (Living Flame 1:4). We do not enjoy this love perfectly here, but the love of the Spirit is the foretaste of eternal life. In 2 Cor 1:21-22 Paul speaks of the Holy Spirit as "arrabon" – this means that the Spirit is the 'downpayment' or 'the first installment' of eternal life. So also in 2 Cor 5:5, the Spirit is the arrabon of the process that is under way in which the believer is being cleansed in a process that will climax in the transformed resurrected body (2 Cor 4:16-5:5). In between, Paul describes the event of conversion as a letter delivered by him, but written in the hearts of the converted by the Spirit (2 Cor 3:3). The Spirit gives life while the letter kills (2 Cor 3:6). The person is called to find love. "The soul's centre is God. When it has reached God with all the capacity of its being and the strength of its operation and inclination, it will have attained its final and deepest centre in God, it will know, love, and enjoy God with all its might." (Living Flame, 1:12). This is the heart of John's teaching. It is the journey we are on to discover our centre and there find the living flame of love.

The Greatest of These...

Paul speaks of the body of Christ which is the faithful. In three important passages he says firstly in
Rom 12:4-8 –

> "For just as in one body we have many members, and all the members do not have the same function, so we all are one body in Christ, and individually members of one another – having charisms which differ in accordance with the grace given to us, whether prophecy in proportion to faith, or service in service, or the one who teaches in teaching, or the one who encourages in encouraging, the one who shares with sincere concern, the one who cares with zest, the one who does acts of mercy with cheerfulness."

1 Cor 12:4-7 –

> "There are diversities of charisms, but the same Spirit.
> There are diversities of service, and the same Lord. There
> are diversities of activities, but the same God, who effects
> all things in everyone. To each is given the manifestation of
> the Spirit for the common good. To one is given a word of
> wisdom through the Spirit, to another a word of knowledge
> in accordance with the same Spirit, to another faith by the
> same Spirit, to another charisms of healing by the one
> Spirit, to another miraculous activities, to another prophecy,
> to another discernment of spirits, to another kinds of
> tongues, to another interpretation of tongues. One and the
> same Spirit effects all these, distributing to each as he wills.
> For just as the body is one and has many members and all
> the members of the body, though many, are one body, so
> also is Christ. For in one Spirit we were all baptised into
> one body, whether Jews or Greeks, whether slaves or free,
> and all watered with the one Spirit. For the body does not
> have one member but many…"

Eph 4:7-16 –

> "But to each of us has been given grace in accordance with
> the measure of the gift of Christ… "He gave gifts to
> humans." … And he gave some as apostles, some as
> prophets, some as evangelists, and some as pastors and
> teachers, to equip the saints for the work of ministry, for the
> upbuilding of the body of Christ…"

The key term in these passages is the Greek word "charisma" translated
as charism. It's very foundation charisma denotes the act of gracious
giving (charizesthai – give graciously). It is a concrete materialisation of
God's grace.[8] It is a product of God's free giving in the Spirit – it is
grace. In Rom 12:4-6 Paul speaks of praxis, which is acting, activity,

---

[8] E. Nardoni, The Concept of Charism in Paul, CBQ (55), 1993, p. 74.

function – the charism is the contribution which the individual member makes to the whole of the community. In 1 Cor 12:4-6 Paul brings out the character of the charism as being for the benefit of others and enabled by the divine power of the Holy Spirit. Charism is also the manifestation of the Spirit for the common good (12:7). Paul later says: "Be zealous for the greater charisms" (12:31) and "Be zealous for what is of the Spirit" (1 Cor 14:1).

In Ephesians 4:7-16 Paul speaks of how we have been given grace (charis). These gifts extend to offices in the local churches (Eph 4:11f). There are apostles, evangelists and prophets. There are teachers. Paul referred to himself as a teacher (1 Cor 4:17; Col 1:28; 3:16). All of these activities are seen as a service to others in the body of Christ. All are gifts of the Holy Spirit. At the end of Chapter 12 and in Chapter 13 we read:

> "Set your mind on the higher gifts. And now I am going to put before you the best way of all.
> Though I command languages both human and angelic – if I speak without love, I am no more than a gong booming or a cymbal clashing. And though I have the power of prophecy, to penetrate all mysteries and knowledge, and though I have all the necessary to move mountains – if I am without love, I am nothing. Though I should give away to the poor all that I possess, and even give up my body to be burned – if I am without love, it will do me no good whatever.
> Love is always patient and kind; love is never jealous; love is not boastful or conceited, it is never rude and never seeks its own advantage, it does not take offence or store up grievances. Love does not rejoice at wrongdoing, but finds its joy in the truth. It is always ready to make allowances, to trust, to hope and to endure whatever comes.
> Love never comes to an end. But if there are prophecies, they will be done away with; if tongues, they will fall silent; and if knowledge, it will be done away with. For we know only imperfectly, and we prophesy imperfectly; but once

perfection comes, all imperfect things will be done away with. When I was a child, I used to talk like a child, and see things as a child does, and think like a child; but now that I have become an adult, I have finished with all childish ways. Now we see only reflections in a mirror, mere riddles, but then we shall be seeing face to face. Now I can know only imperfectly; but then I shall know just as fully as I am myself known.

As it is, these remain: faith, hope nd love, the three of them; and the greatest of them is love.

(1 Cor 12:31-13:13)

Paul says "without love I am nothing" (13:2). This is a stark statement and is a salutary reminder to us, not just to the early Corinthian community. We look at productivity, mission statements, but we never look at love or indeed the might of the great un-loving we see all around us. In 13:1-3 Paul presents himself as a model, but he points out that if he lacks love, all he has said and done is of no worth. Extraordinary gifts, grand abilities and skills, extravagant attitude – all these are emptied of value if love is lacking. So often people are judged on what they produce. Even in religious life and in the churches so much hinges on productivity – how can we look after masses, services and so many other needs. If someone is sick or old then they are often made feel worthless. At the end of the day we will be judged on love (John of the Cross). Rather than define love Paul goes on to personify love. The verbs used all show what love is and point out what is lacking in the Corinthian community and even in Paul himself at times. The only person who fulfills this picture of love is Jesus himself. He is present in the Spirit to lead us to a life of love as described by Paul. Love waits with patience and while waiting it is kind and merciful (13:4). Love is not jealous or boastful, not puffed up, not behaving disgracefully, not seeking its own purposes, not becoming irritated, not keeping score of wrongs, and not taking pleasure in unrighteousness (13:4f). Love passes over all things in silence and endures all things (13:7). Forgiveness is needed to maintain mutual relationships. In 1 Cor 8:3 Paul said: "If someone loves God, then that person is known by God". Love is a two-way street and is true of us and God. God loves us and we are called to love in turn. We can enter, each individually, into an I-thou relationship with God with the Holy Spirit as the love that unites us. He is also like the air that we breathe. In prayer he is with us and in us as we pray and he carries our prayer to God the Father. Love believes all things and hopes all things (13:7). Faith and a right relationship with God is the basis on which we hope for the future, because through faith we know God's redemption in the present and in hope we await for God to complete the work he has begun. It is believing in a spirit of openness. Paul says in 2 Cor 5:7, "We walk through faith not through sight". We live in trust with the God who is for us (Rom 8:31).

Love never ends or fails. Tongues and prophecy pass, but love doesn't because God's eternal love is the ground for all human loving. The love we share in the present is just a pale reflection of the love that we will see in the end-times. We are on a pilgrimage from being children in the faith as the Corinthians were (3:1) to that time of maturity when we see God face to face (13:10). Then Paul says he will exchange his own partial knowledge for a full knowing as he, in turn, is known by God (13:12). We only know love in part and the future that awaits puts the "now" in perspective: "But now remain faith, hope and love, these three and the greatest of these is love" (13:13). Paul often groups these together (cf Rom 5:1-5; Gal 5:5-6; Col 1:4f; 1 Thess 1:3; 5:8). Faith, the right relation to God, makes love possible (Gal 5:6). Hope ends when that for which one hopes is achieved. Love is eternal and is greater than all the gifts the Corinthians admire, but which are in fact transient. It is love that builds up (1 Cor 8:1). The Corinthians had become fixated on gifts and who was the most gifted while neglecting love.

Paul's hymn to love is a call for the community to place love at the centre of its life. The love celebrated in this hymn comes from God and is revealed in Jesus. The Holy Spirit, the living flame of love, enables us to share in this life of love. By becoming one with Jesus in the Spirit we learn love.

In stanza 2 of the 'Living Flame of Love' John of the Cross says:

"O sweet cautery,
O delightful wound!
O gentle hand! O delicate touch
That tastes of eternal life
And pays every debt!
In killing you changed death to life."

The cautery is the Holy Spirit, the hand is the Father and the touch is the Son. The presence of the Trinity brings blessings and love to the soul. Death is changed to life because all members of the Trinity work together. The fire produces a wound when it is applied. It is the wound of love and is only cured by love (Living Flame 2:7). In the end this love produces health in that it cures the soul. The Father wishes to bring life. "For you, O divine life, never kill unless to give life, never wound unless to heal. When you chastise your touch is gentle,... You have wounded me in order to cure me, O divine hand, and you have put to death in me what made me lifeless..." The touches of love are foretastes of eternal life. Even now we possess God through a union of love in the Holy Spirit. The death John refers to in the poem is his old self. Now he is a new creation in God through Jesus by the power of the Holy Spirit.

Thérèse of Lisieux:

Thérèse was a Carmelite nun (1873-1897). During her life as a Carmelite she longed to find her own special vocation. It was while reading this part of St. Paul (1 Cor 13) that she had a moment of revelation. Here is Thérèse's description of how she found her vocation, from her book "The Story of a Soul". Chapter 13 gave Thérèse a light, "Love is the most excellent way that leads to God." She had found her answer:

"At last my mind was at rest... CHARITY gave me the key to my vocation. I understood that the Church had a body made up of different members, the most necessary and most noble of all could not be lacking, and so I understood that the Church had a heart, and that this heart was BURNING

WITH LOVE. I understood that it was LOVE ALONE that made the Church's members act, and that if love ever became extinct, apostles would not preach the Gospel, martyrs would refuse to shed their blood. I understood that LOVE CONTAINED ALL VOCATIONS, THAT LOVE WAS EVERYTHING, THAT IT EMBRACED ALL TIME AND ALL PLACES. IN A WORD, THAT IT IS ETERNAL!

Then, in the excess of my ecstatic joy, I cried out: O Jesus, my love, at last I have found my vocation. MY VOCATION IS LOVE!

Yes, I have found my place in the Church and it is you, O my God, who have given me this place – in the heart of the Church, my mother, I shall be LOVE. Thus I shall be everything – and thus my dream will be fulfilled!!!

(MsB, 3v°)

Thérèse's inspiration was truly insightful. Very often the heart of love, which is the heart of Jesus inflamed by the Holy Spirit, is forgotten and we get bogged down in innumerable discussions and other questions. Thérèse spent her life on earth in prayer for those who felt the might of the world's great unloving. After her death a steady stream of souls have known the power of her love. She brought to the mind of the world the words spoken by St. Paul in 1 Cor 13. She says in her poem "Living on Love":

"Living on love is banishing every fear,
Every moment of past faults,
I see no imprint of my sins.
In a moment love has burned everything...
Divine Flame, O very sweet Blaze!
I make my home in your hearth.
In your fire I gladly sing:
I live on Love..."

(PN 17:6)

Thérèse leads others "to know the love of Christ which is beyond knowledge" (Eph 3:19). By reading and praying the scriptures she came to live the message in her life.

Thérèse spent the last eighteen months of her life in deep pain. She was in communion of Spirit with the suffering servant, Jesus Christ. She shared his prayer on the cross and in the descent into hell. She also was in union with all the broken and all the lonely people of this world. After her death many people came to know of her and many were healed of their pain. St. Paul said of his ministry, "death is at work in us but life in you" (2 Cor 4:12). This was true of Thérèse and the living Jesus to whom she bears testimony. Jesus is the wounded healer.

Paul and Karl Barth (1886-1968):

Karl Barth was a Swiss reformed theologian described by Pope Pius XII as the most important Christian theologian since St. Thomas Aquinas. When Barth was told this he quipped that this proved the Pope was infallible! During his training he studied liberal theology. Part of the methodology of liberal Protestantism was the use of enlightenment sciences to understand the Bible and Christianity. Friedrich Schleiermacher (1768-1834) was regarded as one of the founders of liberal Christianity. He claimed that religious experience was introspective and that the truest experience of God was "a feeling of absolute dependence".[9]

After Barth's training and a two year assistantship in Geneva, Barth became the pastor of a congregation in the small industrial village of Safenwil, Switzerland. He served there for 10 years. However a significant change occurred in October 1914. He discovered that ninety-three German intellectuals had signed a "horrible manifesto" justifying the war policy of Kaiser Wilhelm II, and among those who signed were his former teachers. Barth felt betrayed. For him it showed the hypocrisy of liberal Protestants, together with their lofty ideals, and it

---

[9] See Alister McGrath, Christian Theology (London: 2011).

also called into question the entire theological tradition that could be traced back to Schleiermacher, who had been something of a hero figure for Barth. Mounting the pulpit became a challenge for Barth and he knew he had to return to the Bible. Another Pastor in a neighbouring village, Eduard Thurneysen, began to meet with Barth. As Barth put it:

> "We made a fresh attempt to learn our theological ABC all over again. More reflectively than ever before, we began reading and interpreting the writings of the Old and New Testaments. And behold they began to speak to us – very differently than we had supposed, we were obliged to hear the school of what was then called 'modern theology'"[10]

Barth turned his attention especially to Paul's letter to the Romans. He challenged the Enlightenment's "turn to the subject", inaugurated by Descartes. Barth said: "It is not the right human thoughts about God which form the content of the Bible, but the right divine thoughts about men".[11] God is the right content of the Bible. The mighty voice of Paul was as if it were new to Barth. For Barth it was the subject matter to which Paul's words bore witness that Barth says were decisive for him. He began to study the letter to the Romans verse by verse and see there a challenge to us in our world. Paul "evidently sees and hears something that is above everything, which is absolutely beyond the range of my observation and the measure of my thought."[12]

This eventually led to the publication of his commentary to the Romans in 1919, Der Römerbrief.[13] Barth's methods caused a stir and set him on a lifelong quest to understand faith. One of his own favourite little books

---

[10] K. Barth, 1982, Concluding Unscientific Postscript on Schleiermacher, p. 264 in the Theology of Schleiermacher (Grand Rapids: 1923/24).

[11] K. Barth, 1978, The Strange New World Within the Bible, p. 28-50 in Karl Barth, The Word of God and the Word of Man (Gloucester, Mass: 1978).

[12] Barth, 1978, Autobiographical Sketches in Karl Barth – Rudolph Bultmann, Letters 1922-1966 (Grand Rapids: 1978).

[13] K. Barth, Der Römerbrief, (Bern: Baschlin, 1919) E.T. K. Barth, Epistle to the Romans (London: 1933).

was "Anselm: Fides Quaerens Intelluctum".[14] He dedicated his life to trying to understand faith, and to make it known. His journey began with St. Paul.

Both Thérèse and Barth bring out an important message. Both placed themselves before the text and in their different ways they allowed themselves hear the word of God and from hearing that word they tried to express that word in their lives. They can serve as a model for us when we are searching. We can place ourselves before the word of God in the words of Paul, prayerfully hear these words and know they are not just addressed, as in the case of Paul, to first century Christian communities, but have their relevance today. In a world without love and a world that is so lonely, Thérèse said "I will be love". That was her vocation. We can pray and read the texts and allow God's word to speak to us. Perhaps what we really lack is the confidence to believe!

[14] K. Barth, Anselm: Fides Quaerens Intellectum (London: 1960).

Chapter 3

'The Crucified God'

Jürgen Moltmann in his 1972 work (English translation 1974) 'The Crucified God' quotes the following harrowing scene from Elie Wiesel's book 'Night'.[1] This is Wiesel's account of Auschwitz of which he was a survivor. Elie Wiesel died on the second of July, 2016.

> The SS hanged two Jewish men and a youth in front of the whole camp. The men died quickly, but the death throes of the youth lasted for half an hour. 'Where is God? Where is he?' someone asked behind me. As the youth still hung in torment in the noose after a long time, I heard the man call again, 'Where is God now?' And I heard a voice in myself answer: 'Where is he? He is here. He is hanging there on the gallows…'

Any other answer would be blasphemy. There cannot be any other Christian answer to the question of this torment. To speak here of a God who could not suffer would make God a demon. To speak here of an absolute God would make God an annihilating nothingness. To speak here of an indifferent God would condemn men to indifference.

'Night' opens in Sighet in 1941. The narrative is sparse and fragmented. The book's narrator is Eliezer, but behind the narrative is Wiesel's own story of Auschwitz and Buchenwald. He confesses to losing his faith:

> "Never shall I forget those flames which consumed my faith forever. Never shall I forget that nocturnal silence that deprived me, for all eternity, of the desire to live. Never shall I forget those moments which murdered my God and

---

[1] see E. Wiesel, Night, (New York: 1960) and J. Moltmann, The Crucified God (London: 1974) p. 273f.

my soul and turned my dreams to dust. Never shall I forget those things, even if I am condemned to live as long as God himself. Never."

(Night, p. 32)

In another part of "Night" he asks:

"Blessed be God's name? Why, but why would I bless him? Every fibre in me rebelled. Because he caused thousands of children to burn in mass graves?"

(Night, p. 64)

David Blumenthal in his disturbing book "Facing the Abusive God"[2] recounts how he found that those who had suffered sexual abuse, especially as children, often felt the same as the survivors of the Holocaust whom he counselled over the years.

In 1988 Elie Wiesel published a novel called "Twilight".[3] Its French title was "Le Crépuscule, au loin". It is a novel with the hero named Raphael Lipkin, a Holocaust survivor. He visits a psychiatric ward called "The Mountain Clinic" where he visits patients who believe themselves to be characters from the Old Testament. The title "Twilight" calls to mind the earlier work entitled "Night". Raphael in engaging with the patients is trying to come to terms with his own memories… He reflects on the beauty, heroism and horrible sadness of the human condition. In the story Raphael meets God himself and he pours out his anger and frustration. He comes to realise that we can create our reality. We can imagine a world of goodness, justice, divine wisdom and, perhaps, make it come to pass. It is not a world that exists, nor by just wishing does it come to pass. There is a deep longing in us for this world. This causes us to hope even in the darkness of the night. This is why the new work is called "Twilight". Vincent Van Gogh, who famously painted the "Starry Night" painting once said: "For my part I know nothing with any

[2] D. Blumenthal, Facing the Abusive God: A Theology of Protest (Louisville: 1993).

[3] E. Wiesel, Twilight (London: 1991) The French edition Le Crépuscule, au loin (Paris: 1987) (Twilight in the Distance) refers more precisely to the end of the book, p. 206.

certainty, but the sight of the stars makes me dream". The epigraph of the book is taken from Mamonides who said "the world cannot exist without madness".

The Cross:

The world Jesus found himself in was in turmoil. There was terrorism (state sponsored and otherwise), puppet kings, groups vying for power and domination. A gentle preacher with a message of peace and forgiveness was an outsider, and as an outsider he was eliminated. Hans Urs Von Balthasar speaks of Jesus being sent by the Father with his mission of reconciliation. His mission and his person are identical. At the heart of Jesus' mission is his "obedience" to the Father. The root of obedience is 'ob-audire' from hearing. His obedience is to do the will of the Father.

According to St. Paul, the Son of God in becoming man, did not "cling to his equality with God but emptied himself (heauton ekenôse), taking the form of a servant" (Phil 2:6f). Behind this 'emptying' of himself is his selfless soul and this reflects the selflessness of the persons in the intra-Trinitarian life of love (Magisterium Paschale, p. 153).

> "The Father, who begets the Son, does not "lose" himself in that act to Another in order only thus to "attain" himself; it is precisely as the One who gives himself that he always is himself. And the Son, too, is always himself by letting himself be begotten and letting the Father have him at his disposal. The Spirit is always himself by seeing his "I" as the "We" of Father and Son, making this expropriation his *propriissimum*. (It is only when we understand this that we escape from the machinery of Hegel's dialectic)."
>
> (TD 3, p. 232)

"No one has ever seen God", says John in his Gospel, "the only Son who is in the bosom of the Father, he has made him known" (John 1:18). The Greek verb here translated as "to make known" means to expound, to explain, to reveal. The Holy Spirit brings us into the unity of love of Father and Son; in this way we come to know Jesus and the things he taught (Jn 16:4-15).

Christ's excess of love made him all the more inclined to suffer. The stronger love is, the more painful are the wounds of co-suffering. He loved those who were alienated and broken and he entered in love into that pain. His was the pain of co-suffering and his co-suffering goes beyond all other suffering for the excess of his love transcends all other suffering of others. His love is total and this is the meaning of kenosis.

In the Gospel of Mark we read the following account of Jesus' agony in Gethsemane:

> "They came to a plot of land called Gethsemane, and he said to his disciples, 'Stay here while I pray.' Then he took Peter and James and John with him. And he began to feel terror and anguish. And he said to them, 'My soul is sorrowful to the point of death. Wait here, and stay awake.' And going on a little further he threw himself on the ground and prayed that, if it were possible, this hour might pass him by. 'Abba, Father!' he said, 'For you everything is possible. Take this cup away from me. But let it be as you, not I, would have it.' He came back and found them sleeping, and he said to Peter, 'Simon, are you asleep? Had you not the strength to stay awake one hour? Stay awake and pray not to be put to the test. The spirit is willing enough, but human nature is weak.' Again he went away and prayed, saying the same words. And once more he came back and found them sleeping, their eyes were so heavy; and they could find no answer for him. He came back a third time and said to them, 'You can sleep on now and have your rest. It is all over. The hour has come. Now the Son of man is to be betrayed into the hands of sinners. Get up! Let us go! My betrayer is not far away.'"

> (Mk 14:32-42)

Jesus asks for friends to be with him but his friends slept. He called out to his Father calling him by the intimate family name 'Abba' but he is silent. Jesus falls into a deep fear (ekthambeisthe), into an anguish of aloneness and deep loneliness (a-demonein, anguish in separation from all). He is led to feel as if dead. It is he hora, the hour (Mk 14:34). Hope in God and the consolation of faith have disappeared from his soul, and he is now filled with doubt and anguish (Isaac of Nineveh). Evagrius of Pontus says that every exertion towards God seems vain. He uses the Greek word akedia, which has the sense of futility, despair and God abandonment. It is an experience of Hell (Mysterium Paschale, p. 77). Karl Barth writes:

> "A *theologia gloriae*, celebrating what Jesus Christ in his Resurrection, received for us, and what he is for us as the Risen One, would have no meaning unless it also contained in itself the *theologia crucis*: the praise of what he has done for us in his death and of what he is for us as the crucified. But no more would an abstract *theologia crucis* have meaning. One cannot celebrate in proper fashion the passion and death of Jesus Christ, if this praise does not already contain in itself the *theologia gloriae*: the praise of him who, in his Resurrection, receives our justice and our life, the One who rose for us from among the dead."
>
> (K. Barth, CD4/1, p. 622)

The death of Jesus is described in stark, sparse terms by St. Mark:

> "When the sixth hour came there was darkness over the whole land until the ninth hour. And at the ninth hour Jesus cried out in a loud voice, 'Eloi, eloi, lama sabachthani?' which means, 'My God, my God, why have you forsaken me?' When some of those who stood by heard this, they said, 'Listen, he is calling on Elijah.' Someone ran and soaked a sponge in vinegar and, putting it on a reed, gave it to him to drink saying, 'Wait! And see if Elijah will come to take him down.' But Jesus gave a loud cry and breathed his last. And the veil of the Sanctuary was torn in two from

top to bottom. The centurion, who was standing in front of him, had seen how he had died, and he said, 'In truth this man was Son of God.'

(Mk 15:33-39)

Jesus cry in Aramaic, '*Eloi, eloi, lama sabachthani*' is taken from Ps 22 and expresses his feelings of abandonment. The giving of vinegar recalls the words of Ps 69:22, "in my thirst they gave me vinegar to drink". Jesus' end is sudden and violent. He gives out a loud scream and dies in agony. His heroism inspires the centurion to recognise God was present in the man Jesus. He echoes the opening of the Gospel (Mk 1:1) "The beginning of the Gospel about Jesus Christ, the Son of God." In Mk 8:29 Peter had made an act of faith that Jesus was the Christ of God, but he did not accept that the Christ of God should suffer. In contrast, the centurion's act of faith takes place at Jesus' death agony.

Yet within three days the one who was dead rose again. The New Testament contains accounts of different people who encountered him. Paul states:

> "Then he appeared to more than five hundred brothers at one time... Then he appeared to James, then to all the apostles. Last of all, as to one untimely born, he appeared also to me."

(1 Cor 15:6-8)

Paul also speaks of Jesus appearing to 'Cephas' (1 Cor 15:3). Jesus rising from the dead is the first-fruits of God's new creation (1 Cor 15:20-58). His resurrection took his apostles completely by surprise. They realise it is by the power of God, the Holy Spirit. God's pneuma (the Greek word for Spirit) accomplishes the resurrection (see Rom 8:1, 1 Pt 3:18). Ephesians 1:19 speaks of God's power raising Jesus. Jesus gives the Spirit who inhabits us as the principle of our adoption as children of God. In the Gospel of Luke Jesus meets two disciples on the road to Emmaus going away from Jerusalem (Lk 24:13-32). When they meet Jesus they find their courage restored and they recognise Jesus in the breaking of bread. They rush back to tell the other disciples about their experience, they are told of the good news of the vision of Peter, but then when Jesus himself appears they take fright and have to be convinced by tangible proofs (Lk 24:33-42). This illustrates the newness of this new event. The resurrection is a Trinitarian event, in it the Father as the "God of the living" (Rom 4:17) awakens the Son from the dead, so that he, now no longer experiencing Godforsakeness but is one in peace with the Father, can send forth God's Spirit into the church (see Mysterium Paschale, p. 257-281). The apostles assembled on Easter-day encounter a Spirit-filled but also corporeal Christ: he breathes his Spirit into them (John 20:22), but he also wants to be touched by them so that no-one will think he is a ghost. The event of the resurrection is real.

For Paul the heart of his teaching lies in the death and the resurrection of Jesus. In Galatians 3:13-14, Christ cursed on the cross shows God fulfilled his promise to bring in the gentiles as Abraham's children. In Colossians (2:6-16) we read:

"So then, as you received Jesus as Lord and Christ, now live your lives in him, be rooted in him and built up on him, held firm by the faith you have been taught, and overflowoing with thanksgiving.
Make sure that no one captivates you with the empty lure of a 'philosophy' of the kind that human beings hand on, based on the principles of this world and not on Christ.
In him, in bodily form, lives divinity in all its fullness, and in him you too find your own fulfillment, in the one who is the head of every sovereignty and ruling force.
In him you have been circumcised, with a circumcision performed, not by human hand, but by the complete stripping of your natural self. This is circumcision according to Christ. You have been buried with him by your baptism; by which, too, you have been raised up with him through your belief in the power of God who raised him from the dead. You were dead, because you were sinners and uncircumcised in body: he has brought you to life with him, he has forgiven us every one of our sins.
He has wiped out the record of our debt to the Law, which

stood against us; he has destroyed it by nailing it to the cross; and he has stripped the sovereignties and the ruling forces, and paraded them in public, behind him in his triumphal procession."

(Col 2:6-16)

Here Paul describes the festivals and times of other festivals and philosophies but Paul reminds the new Christians they belong to Christ. They are told to carry on in the fashion they had begun in and they are called to cultivate their relationship with Jesus. They are to be loyal to the tradition passed on to them (e.g. 1 Cor 15:1-3; Gal 1:9; 1 Thess 4:1; 2 Thess 3:6). "Walk in him" (see also Col 1:10) is the injunction. 'Walking' (halakhah) is a Hebrew idea of following the ways of God; now this is applied to Jesus. The readers are warned to be on their guard against those who would lead them from their faith. Through their incorporation into Christ the believers are filled with the Holy Spirit and live in a totally new way. This new power and way of life has been opened up by Christ's resurrection.

Yet the resurrected one is the crucified one. In the first letter to the Corinthians we read: "We are preaching a crucified Christ: to the Jews an obstacle they cannot get over, to the Gentiles foolishness, but to those who have been called, a Christ who is both the power of God and the Wisdom of God" (1 Cor 1:23f). God's power is used and expressed differently than the world we live in. God destroys the wisdom of the wise of this world (see 1 Cor 1:19, Isa 29:14 and Ps 33:10). God's weakness is stronger than human strength (1 Cor 1:25). In the communities of Paul's time many (especially the Jewish converts) would have heard the following from the Book of Deuteronomy: "Cursed is everyone who has been hanged on a tree" (Deut 21:33). Galatians 3:13 says: "Christ redeemed us from the curse of the Law by being cursed for our sake since it says: anyone hanged is a curse." These texts show how great a shock it was to preach a crucified messiah.

The Son being sent "in the very likeness of human flesh" (Rom 8:3) deals with sin by his death. Similarly Galatians 4:4-5 tells us he was sent, "born of a woman, born under the law, in order that he might redeem those under the law…" He accepted death, death on a cross (Phil 2:7-8). In the second letter to the Corinthians we read:

> "For the love of God overwhelms us when we consider if one man died for all, then all have died; his purpose in dying for all humanity was that those who live should live not any more for themselves, but for him who died and was raised to life for them. From now onwards, then, we will not consider anyone by human standards; even if we were once familiar with Christ by human standards, we do not know him in that way any longer."
>
> (2 Cor 5:14ff)

The flow of love comes from God through Christ in the power of the Holy Spirit. It is love that builds up (1 Cor 8:1). Christ has died for all so that all might live… 'Christ died for the ungodly' (Rom 5:6), 'Christ died for us' (Rom 5:8) [see also 1 Cor 8:11; 15:3; 1 Thess 5:10]. Because he sees believers dying with Christ, a way of saying leaving the old ways behind (see Rom 5:15; 6:3-6), Paul says that all have died but we are transformed into new beings by the power of Christ's death and resurrection. It is started with us and spread and in the end-times encompasses the whole of the universe. We are now to live a life with "faith working through love" (Gal 5:6). "All who belong to Christ Jesus have crucified self with all its passions and its desires. Since we are living by the Spirit, let our behaviour be guided by the Spirit…" (Gal 5:24f).

In the letter to the Philippians Paul writes of the importance the event of meeting Jesus has had for him:

> "But what were once my assets I now through Christ Jesus count as losses. Yes, I will go further: because of the supreme advantage of knowing Christ Jesus my Lord, I count everything else as loss. For him I have accepted the loss of all other things, and look on them all as filth if only I can gain Christ and be given a place in him, with the uprightness I have gained not from the Law, but through

faith in Christ, an uprightness from God, based on faith, that I may come to know him and the power of his resurrection, and partake of his sufferings by being moulded to the pattern of his death, striving towards the goal of resurrection from the dead. Not that I have secured it already, nor yet reached my goal, but I am still pursuing it in the attempt to take hold of the prize for which Christ Jesus took hold of me. Brothers, I do not reckon myself as having taken hold of it; I can only say that forgetting all that lies behind me, and straining forward to what lies in front, I am racing towards the finishing-point to win the prize of God's heavenly call in Christ Jesus. So this is the way in which all of us who are mature should be thinking, and if you are still thinking differently in any way, then God has yet to make this matter clear to you. Meanwhile, let us go forward from the point we have each attained.
Brothers be united in imitation me."

(Phil 3:7-16)

Paul has just been boasting of his achievements as a Pharisee, but now he sees all this as loss compared to knowing Jesus. The things that are important for him now are being found in Christ (v.9) and knowing him (v.8). Paul uses the word skybala to describe the past things of his life. The word can be translated as "rubbish" or "refuse". Christ's resurrection is here seen as the source of power in the believer. In his own life Paul describes how he follows Christ and shares in his sufferings so as to know the power of the resurrection. Being conformed to Christ's death is ongoing in the life of the believer (2 Cor 4:10-12) and the attaining of the resurrection from the dead lies in the future. The resurrection and bringing to completion of the salvation of the world for the believer lies in the future. Christ's resurrection has taken place and on this we base our hope for our resurrection and that of the whole universe.

In St. John of the Cross's 'Living Flame of Love' he describes how the person is transformed inwardly by the power of the Spirit.

"The soul feels its ardour strengthen and increase and its love become so refined in this ardour that seemingly there flow seas of loving fire within it, reaching to the heights and depths of the earthly and heavenly spheres, imbuing all with love. It seems to it that the entire universe is a sea of love in which it is engulfed, for conscious of the living point or centre of love within itself, it is unable to catch sight of the boundaries of this love"

(Living Flame, 2:10)

St. Francis meditated on the figure of Jesus who embodied this love, the wounds of Jesus appeared on his body and he felt as if he were living in the vastness of the sea of God's love. When his soul was wounded with love by the five wounds, their effect extended to his body, and these wounds were impressed on the body, which was wounded just as his soul was wounded with love (Living Flame, 2:13). John compares Jesus to the "gentle breeze" of 1 Kgs 19:11-12. "O gentle breeze, since you are a delicate and mild breeze, tell us: How do you, the Word, the Son of God, touch mildly and gently, since you are so awesome and mighty?" (Living Flame, 2:17). God in Jesus reaches out in love to heal the broken, comfort the sorrowful and bring the lonely into communion with him in "this sea of love". The Holy Spirit leads to the possession of God through the union of love (Living Flame, 2:32). This 'possession' is like the cry of the bride in the Song of Songs: "I am my beloved and he is mine" (Song 2:16)

In 1 Cor 15:45 Paul says: "The first Adam became a living soul (see Gen 2:7), the last Adam became a life-giving spirit". Making alive is a phrase that refers to the Holy Spirit. This association goes back to Gen 2:7 itself: "God breathed into Adam's (man's) nostrils the breath of life." In Job 33:4 we read: "The Spirit of God has made me and the breath of the Almighty gives me life" and in Ps 104:29f: "When you take away your breath, they die and return to the dust. When you send forth your spirit they are created." There is also the vision of Ezekiel 37 of the Spirit breathing on the dead bones (of Israel) "that they may live" (Ez 37:9f). In Paul himself he speaks of the life-giving function of the Holy Spirit (Rom 8:11 and 2 Cor 36). In Rom 8:2 he speaks of him as the "Spirit of Life".

Another distinction of the work of the Spirit in Paul is that the believer can call out in prayer "Abba, Father". This shows we are adopted children (Rom 8:14-17). The Spirit's inspiration is moulded by the confession Jesus is Lord (1 Cor 12:3). The work of the Spirit transforms Christians into the likeness of the divine (2 Cor 3:18) which is Christ (2 Cor 4:4). Hence the Spirit is now known as "the spirit of Christ" (Rom 8:9), "the spirit of God's Son" (Gal 4:6), "the spirit of Jesus Christ" (Phil 1:19). The point is that Paul saw all of God's purpose for humankind as focussed on the resurrection of the crucified. The Adam (man) of God's purpose is the risen Christ, so also he focuses the life-giving power of the Spirit, by which this life purpose is to be extended to embrace those represented by the last Adam. Christ is experienced as working in and through the Spirit. The Spirit is the medium of Christ's union with his own. This helps us see the meaning of the last Adam as a life-giving Spirit (1 Cor 15:45).

For Von Balthasar the love of created beauty and art can help us understand what it is to be enraptured by Christ. As Incarnate Love, he is not merely one subject of beauty among others, but rather the perfection and measure of all worldly beauty (GL1:177, 431f). Something of beauty uplifts us and expands our openness to reality (GL1:118). It reminds us human beings of our dignity, made as we are in God's image and called as we are to the divine likeness. Jesus is the image of the unseen God (Colossians 1:15). When we contemplate him in his mysteries, the Spirit of love is the medium between us. As we contemplate him in the scriptures we come to know him and the power of his love. We are drawn into that love by the medium of the Holy Spirit. Paul's words are a source for our contemplation and in silence we can let ourselves be loved:

> Paul's prayer
> This, then, is what I pray, kneeling before the Father, from whom every fatherhood, in heaven or on earth, takes its name. In the abundance of his glory may he, through his Spirit, enable you to grow firm in power with regard to your inner self, so that Christ may live in your hearts through faith, and then, planted in love and built on love, with all

God's holy people you will have the strength to grasp the breadth and the length, the height and the depth; so that, knowing the love of Christ, which is beyond all knowledge, you may be filled with the utter fullness of God.

Glory be to him whose power, working in us, can do infinitely more than we can ask or imagine; glory be to him from generation to generation in the Church and in Christ Jesus, for ever and ever. Amen.

(Eph 3:14-21)

We are close to God and special to him. His prayer is that we come to know the love of God in Christ which is beyond measure and be "filled with the utter fullness of God." By contemplating the Christ of God we enter into that sea of love, the medium of the Spirit.

The Failures of Love:

For many people their lives are more marked by the failures of love. We have so many victims of abuse, violence and wars. There are victims of torture and displacement. This pain is too great, so people distract themselves frantically to keep these lonely people out of sight, out of mind. Yet inner loneliness stalks them and all must at some stage face themselves. The might of the world's great unloving has many victims.

Vincent Van Gogh knew this loneliness. He looked at the figure of the lonely and crucified one and he felt he was accepted there and that he was loved. He poured out his pain in his paintings but he did so with love, so the person beholding could feel the love and accept themselves. St. Paul said "Anyone who attaches to the Lord is one Spirit with him" (1 Cor 6:17). It was Nietzsche who said of the abyss of evil, fear and destruction: if we continue to stare long enough into the abyss, the abyss will stare back at us. The might of unloving causes us to stare into the abyss.

Jürgen Moltmann (b. 1926) is a German theologian. Yet he was born with little or no religion. His family might go to church once a year. He was born in Hamburg. As a young man he thought of becoming a scientist. Einstein was his hero and he was fascinated by the theories of relativity. He was conscripted during the war and he took with him as reading material Goethe's poems and the works of Nietzsche. He was then taken into the full army and became a prisoner of war in 1945. For the next three years he was moved from camp to camp. Eventually he ended up near Kilmarnock in Scotland. He was filled with depression and as more and more information came out about the concentration camps he felt an acute shame. He also wrestled with the question: "why did he survive? Why did the man beside him die?"

One day a well-meaning chaplain came and:

> "after a brief address distributed Bibles. Some of us would certainly rather have had a few cigarettes. I read the book in the evenings without much understanding until I came upon the psalms of lament in the Old Testament. Psalm 39 caught my attention particularly:
>
> I am dumb and must eat up my suffering within myself.
> My life is as nothing before thee [Luther's version].
> Hear my prayer, O Lord, and give ear to my cry.
> Hold not thou thy peace at my tears,
> for I am a stranger with thee, and a sojourner, as all my fathers were.
>
> That was an echo from my own soul, and it called that soul to God. I didn't experience any sudden illumination, but I came back to these words every evening. Then I read Mark's Gospel as a whole and came to the story of the passion; when I heard Jesus' death cry 'My God, why have you forsaken me?' I felt growing within me the conviction: this is someone who understands you completely, who is with you in your cry to God and has felt the same forsakenness you are living in now. I began to understand the assailed, forsaken Christ because I knew that he understood me. The divine brother in need, the companion

on the way, who goes with you through this 'valley of the shadow of death', the fellow-sufferer who carries you, with your suffering. I summoned up the courage to live again, and I was slowly but surely seized by a great hope for the resurrection into God's 'wide space where there is no more cramping'. This perception of Christ did not come all of a sudden and overnight, either, but it became more and more important for me, and I read the story of the passion again and agin, for preference in the Gospel of Mark."[4]

It was like Elijah again (1 Kgs 19:12ff) he found God: the soft, still voice and then he turned towards theology, abandoning his dreams of science. He began his studies in England in Norton Camp. Then he returned to Germany, studied in Göttingen and was a pastor in Wasserhorst. Thus began his theological career. He had an initial fascination with Barth, but then began to read Bonhoeffer and entered a dialogue with the Marxist, Ernst Bloch. He asked Bloch once was he an atheist: Bloch replied with a twinkle in his eye, "I am an atheist for God's sake" (A Broad Place, p. 79). This resulted in the publication eventually of Moltmann's "Theology of Hope".[5] Another incident Moltmann speaks about in developing his thoughts about hope. He was a theologian who was involved. He travelled to Poland in1963 in a meeting trying to bring reconciliation. He describes his experience of walking through the sites of former concentration camps:

"The most deeply emotional experience was to walk through the Maidanek concentration and death camp, near Lublin. The plank beds in the barracks were the last resting places of starving and tormented men, women, and children. Behind glass lay the little shoes of the murdered Jewish children, and hair that had been cut off from the gassed women. We saw the pits in which more than 10,000 people had been shot on a single day. At the time I wanted to sink into the ground for shame, and would have

[4] see N.T. Wright, Paul and the Faithfulness of God (London: 2013).

[5] J. Moltmann, A Broad Place (London: 2007) p. 30.

suffocated in the presence of the mass murder, if on one of the roads through the camp I had not suddenly had a vision. I looked into the world of the resurrection and saw all these dead men, women, and children coming towards me. Since then I have known that God's history with Auschwitz and Maidanek has not been broken off, but that it goes further with the victims and with the perpetrators. Without hope for the 'new earth in which righteousness dwells' (2 Peter 3:13), this earth, which has suffered Treblinka and Maidanek, would be unendurable."

(A Broad Place, p. 84)

His book touched a chord in many hearts. There had not been a great emphasis on Jesus' victory over death in the resurrection and God's will that we all share in his victory. The book was very successful. In the "Theology of Hope" he says God becomes the companion on the way and is a fellow-sufferer with all his people in the exile of this world. The Shekinah (God's abiding presence) is a divine presence that fills every life. He quotes St. Paul who said: "For all the promises of God find their yes in him" (2 Cor 1:20). That affirmation was the reason for interpreting the resurrection of Jesus from the dead as God's final and universal promise of the new creation of all things. The fulfillment of the promise initially touches only Jesus, but God raised him from the dead so that he might be the first-fruits of all who have fallen asleep and the leader of the universe[6] (see 1 Cor 15:35-48). The fulfillment of the promise becomes universal – for the living and the dead and the whole of creation. Without the coming kingdom of God's glory and the eternal life of the future world, God's raising of Jesus from the dead has no significance, but without his raising, the hope of Christians has no Christian foundation.

> "Now if Christ is proclaimed as raised from the dead, how can some of you be saying that there is no resurrection of the dead? If there is no resurrection of the dead, then Christ cannot have been raised either, and if Christ has not been

---

[6] He develops this more in The Way of Jesus Christ (London: 1990).

raised, then our preaching is without substance, and so is our faith. What is more, we have proved to be false witnesses to God, for testifying against God that he raised Christ to life when he did not raise him – if it is true that the dead are not raised. For, if the dead are not raised, neither is Christ; and if Christ has not been raised, your faith is pointless and you have not, after all, been released from your sins. In addition, those who have fallen asleep in Christ are utterly lost. If our hope in Christ has been for this life only, we are of all people the most pitiable.

In fact, however, Christ has been raised from the dead, as the first-fruits of all who have fallen asleep. As it was by one man that death came, so through one man has come the resurrection of the dead. Just as all die in Adam, so in Christ all will be brought to life; but all of them in their proper order: Christ the first-fruits, and next, at his coming, those who belong to him. After that will come the end, when he will hand over the kingdom to God the Father, having abolished every principality, every ruling force and power. For he is to be king until he has made his enemies his footstool, and the last of the enemies to be done away with is death, for he has put all things under his feet. But when it is said everything is subjected, this obviously cannot include the One who subjected everything to him. When everything has been subjected to him, then the Son himself will be subjected to the One who has subjected everything to him, so that God may be all in all."

(1 Cor 15:12-28)

Here Paul addresses the general view of the resurrection from the dead. Christ is the first-fruits and where he is we hope to follow. Paul says "I die daily" (15:31) meaning he suffers but his hope is in God's victory in Jesus. The future hope of believers influences our conduct and world-view in the present. If the dead are not raised "let us eat and drink because tomorrow we die" (15:32 quoting Isa 22:13). No, Jesus is raised and we are promised that we too will be raised to be with him. God's promise finds its yes in Jesus (2 Cor 1:20).

In 1968 during a conference on "The Theology of Hope and the New Task of Theology" in Duke University, Martin Luther King Jr. was assassinated. In the same year there was student unrest in the world, especially in Paris. The Vietnam War was continuing. The Prague spring was brought to a violent end when the Russians invaded Czechoslovakia. The world was in ferment. In Ireland the "troubles" were just beginning. All these events caused Moltmann to look at the crucified one. The crucified one is the risen one and in 1974 his work "The Crucified God" appeared (the German original appeared in 1972). He followed this with "The Church in the Power of the Spirit" (1977) and his 1992 work "The Spirit of Life: A Universal Affirmation". He wrote other works in between but here is where I find him wrestling with the evil in the world. In "Theology of Hope" he wrote:

> "Thus the Spirit is the power to suffer in participation in the mission and the love of Jesus Christ, and is in this suffering the passion for what is possible, for what is coming and promised in the future of life, of freedom and of resurrection."
>
> (Theology of Hope, p. 212)

Jesus, in his love, suffered the experience of godforsakenness of the world so that the world would no longer be godforsaken. Jesus suffered the abandonment by the Father so that those who feel abandoned might know they are held close to God. The Father suffers in his way – in his grief over the death and rejection of his Son. The Father in compassion suffers his Son's pain and rejection. It is because of love that God suffers the contradictions of a godless world. In his love he is present with the godless and the godforsaken, and therefore reaches them with his love.

The event of the Cross includes the whole of suffering and sinful reality within the love of God. Moltmann says that Jesus accomplishes this by his identification with the godforsaken and the godless. The Spirit is the love which unites the Father and the Son even in their experience of being apart. The Spirit flows out from the event of the Cross to include all reality in the divine love. The Spirit he says "is the unconditional and therefore boundless love, which proceeds from the grief of the Father and the dying of the Son and reaches forsaken men in order to create in them the possibility and the force of a new life." (Crucified God, p. 245). The Cross is where God identifies himself with those that contradict him in order to overcome the contradiction by suffering in love. For Moltmann God is affected and moved by his creation and the fate of his children. What really happens on the Cross, says Moltmann, is that the persons of the Trinity are open to include the world, the fallen world, within them. We do not yet see God's victory. We live in the in-between times: the Spirit continues to mediate between the history of Jesus and the eschatological future (the end-times when God will be all-in-all [1 Cor 15:24] and we will experience his full victory in the new creation). God is glorified in the resurrection of Jesus, so we wait for God's glorification when all creation will be caught up in the divine life.

We can conceive of the Spirit's personal relation to the Father and the Son by bringing ourselves into the picture. The Spirit inspires our relation to the Father and the Son. He is the Spirit of love who unites us with the Father and the Son. "In the Spirit God dwells in men himself" (The Kingdom of God, p. 104). In the Spirit of Life Moltmann says we can know the Spirit as "presence" and counterpart (we come to know as in a 'face to face' relationship) (Spirit of Life, p. 304). We are drawn into the love that is the heart of the Trinity (Spirit of Life, p. 305).

Von Balthasar and Moltmann agree on many points. Von Balthasar uses the term "the darkness of God" (TD5, p. 265ff) to describe what Moltmann calls the suffering of God the Father. He discusses Moltmann's 'Crucified God' to show the differences between them (TD5, p. 227ff). What is important for Von Balthasar is to keep in mind that God is "totally other". Von Balthasar says that the Spirit of truth introduces the believer into the relationship between Son and Father (Jn 16:13) and this is the meaning of absolute truth.

John of the Cross tries to express this union by using the poetic image of fire, of branding with a branding iron. This causes a wound, that unlike a bodily wound, can only be healed by being deepened "until the soul at last is one single wound of love… and so is healed by love" (Flame 2:7). Love is felt as an endless ocean and its "beginning and middle seem to be in the soul itself." (Flame 2:7). This is the indwelling that John speaks of in John 14:21-24. St. Paul reminds us, the Spirit dwells in us (1 Cor 6:19). As the Spirit dwelt in the Shekinah, God's presence in the Temple, so now he dwells in us.

Chapter 4

Anxiety and Loneliness

Anxiety is an emotion characterized by an unpleasant state of inner turmoil, often accompanied by nervous behaviour, such as pacing back and forth, somatic complaints and rumination. "Footfalls" was a play written by Samuel Beckett and we experience the anxiety of the heroine as she paces back and forth. Anxiety can be the dread of annihilation. Anxiety is not the same as fear which is a response to a real or perceived threat, whereas anxiety is the expression of the expectation of a future threat. Anxiety is a fear of fear, uneasiness and worry, usually generalised and unfocussed and can lead to an anxiety neurosis. It is often accompanied by muscular tension, restlessness, fatigue and problems in concentration. Anxiety can be appropriate but if it takes over can lead to an anxiety disorder. The philosopher Soren Kierkegaard in the "Concept of Anxiety" (1844)[1] described anxiety or dread as being associated with the dizziness of freedom and suggested the possibility for positive resolution of anxiety through the self-conscious exercise of responsibility and choosing. In "Art and the Artist" the psychologist Otto Rank wrote that the psychological trauma of birth was the pre-eminent human symbol of existential anxiety and encompasses the creative person's fear of – and desire for – separation, individuation and differentiation.[2] The theologian Paul Tillich[3] characterised existential anxiety as the state in which a being is aware of its possible nonbeing. He spoke of the spiritual anxiety of the age as that of the anxiety of meaninglessness and emptiness. He felt we should accept this anxiety as being part of the human condition. To suppress or deny it leads to frustration and investing oneself in strange causes. The psychiatrist Viktor Frankl,[4] the author of "Man's Search for Meaning", says that

---

[1] S. Kierkegaard, The Concept of Anxiety (New York: 2014).

[2] O. Rank, Art and the Artist (New York: 1989).

[3] P. Tillich, The Courage to Be (Chicago: 1952).

[4] V. Frankl, Man's Search for Meaning (London: 2006).

when a person is faced with extreme mortal dangers, the most basic of all human wishes is to find a meaning in life to combat the trauma of nonbeing as death nears. Jim Morrison of the 'Doors' wrote about the feelings of anxiety in the song "People are Strange". He says:

> "People are strange when you're a stranger
> Faces look ugly when you're alone
> - - - - - - -
> Streets are uneven, when you're down
> When you're strange
> Faces come out of the rain
> When you're strange
> No one remembers your name
> When you're strange
> When you're strange"
>
> (from the album 'Strange Days', 1967)

I know that place of feeling alone, out of place – a stranger in a strange land 'desperately in need of some stranger's hand'. All the world seems strange and I have become a stranger even to myself. Loneliness is the illness of our days.

Abraham Joshua Herschel (+1972) is someone who has inspired me. He lived in Germany during the rise of the Nazis and Hitler. He experienced the evil of the rejection of his people. He studied philosophy in the University of Berlin and he was impressed with the great systems of thought of the great philosophers.

> "I came with great hunger to the University of Berlin to study philosophy. I looked for a system of thought, for the depth of the spirit, for the meaning of existence. Erudite and profound scholars gave courses in logic, epistemology, esthetics, ethics, and metaphysics. ... Yet in spite of the intellectual power and honesty which I was privileged to witness, I became increasingly aware of the gulf that separated my views from those held at the university.... To them, religion was a feeling. To me, religion included the

insights of the Torah which is a vision of man from the point of view of God. They spoke of God from the point of view of man. To them God was an idea, a postulate of reason. They granted Him the status of being a logical possibility. But to assume that He had existence would have been a crime against epistemology."

(Man's Quest for God, p. 94f)[5]

The result of this confrontation was Heschel's attempt to examine the classical documents of Judaism anew to discover their relevance for the contemporary world. In this enterprise he made use of the conceptual tools of contemporary philosophy, especially the techniques of phenomenology. Heschel turned towards the prophets, using comparative religion, literary, phenomenological and theological perspectives.

He received a visa to America the week before Hitler invaded Poland. he describes himself as a brand plucked from the fire (Zech 3:1-2).

"I speak as a member of a congregation whose founder was Abraham, and the name of my rabbi is Moses.
I speak as a person who was able to leave Warsaw, the city in which I was born, just six weeks before the disaster began. My destination was New York, it would have been Auschwitz or Treblinka. I am a brand plucked from the fire, in which my people was burned to death. I am a brand plucked from the fire of an altar of Satan on which millions of human lives were exterminated to evil's greater glory, and on which so much else was consumed: the divine image of so many human beings, many people's faith in the God of justice and compassion, and much of the secret and power of attachment to the Bible bred and cherished in the hearts of men for nearly two thousand years."[6]

[5] A.J. Heschel, Man's Quest for God: Studies in Prayer and Symbolism (New York: 1954).

[6] A.J. Heschel, No Religion is an Island, Union Seminary Quarterly Review 21 (January 1966), p. 117.

The world he found was cruel. He lost his family in the death camps and he found it hard to communicate to the world the plight of European Jewry.

In his work he began to look at what it means to be human in a world where much of what is human has been lost. He sees our age as an age that is losing any understanding of what it means to be human. Ours is an age that has forgotten how to pray, how to think, how to cry. We have exchanged holiness for convenience, loyalty for success, love for power, wisdom for information and tradition for fashion. (Man's Quest for God, p. 150). We legislate against murder yet wars are raged with ferocity and whole peoples are slaughtered. People are looked upon for their usefulness.

He says that it is essential to being human that one learns to stand alone. For the one who seeks to be authentically human, what other resource is there than the occasional withdrawal from the world's glaring and deceitful eyes? Solitude implies a period of rest and recovery from the incursions of society's hysteria. Then we return to society. "Human is he who is concerned with other selves."[7] This comes to pass in a world of cruel indifference where the selfish are rewarded and the vulnerable crushed. Indifference and harshness of heart is increasing daily and many are left lonely.

It was usual one time to seek in religion an answer to these problems. Here Heschel has some prophetic things to say about religion. He says:

> "It is customary to blame secular science and antireligious philosophy for the eclipse of religion in modern society. It would be more honest to blame religion for its own defeats. Religion declined not because it was refuted, but because it became irrelevant, dull, oppressive, insipid. When faith is completely replaced by creed, worship by discipline, love by habit; when the crisis of today is ignored because of the splendor of the past; when faith becomes an heirloom rather

[7] A.J. Heschel, Man is Not Alone: A Philosophy of Religion (New York: 1951).

than a living fountain; when religion speaks only in the name of authority rather than with the voice of compassion, its message becomes meaningless.

Religion is an answer to ultimate questions. The moment we become oblivious to ultimate questions, religion becomes irrelevant, and its crisis sets in. The primary task of religious thinking is to rediscover the questions to which religion is the answer, to develop a degree of sensitivity to the ultimate questions which its ideas and acts are trying to answer."[8]

This is an experience of religion where compassion has been lacking. A lack of compassion and a dearth of humanity mark many people's experiences. As an outgrowth of the lack of compassion and the dearth of humanity comes abuse. Many have experienced sexual abuse and many of these people were children. Instead of the Church being a safe place, for many it has become a place of nightmares. They are denied the very consolation they need. Yet there always remains a spiritual underground where there have always been a few brave souls to fight. The Spirit is a still small voice, and the masters of vulgarity use loudspeakers. The question we face is do we matter? Are we lonely in a vast universe? Is there no-one to collect the tears, soothe the pain, understand the agony of the innocent, the poor, the sorrowing? Is there no Presence worth living for, worth dying for, no way of living that is compatible with this Presence. We are a need of God. He is the Presence who invites us into communion with him. We are his investment and we are called to be transformed in him by the Love of the Spirit.

The Prophets:

Rabbi Heschel says: "We must first peer into the darkness, feel strangled and entombed in the hopelessness of living without God, before we are ready to feel the presence of His living light." (God in Search of Man, p. 140). Heschel found the world a dark place and it was his faith that

[8] A.J. Heschel, God in Search of Man: A Philosophy of Judaism (New York: 1955).

God in his silence still listens to his cry, who could stand such agony? (The Hiding God, EW p. 84). There is God who hears. As Psalm 31 says:

> "I am weary with my mourning;
> every night I flood my bed with tears;
> I drench my couch with my weeping
> My eyes waste away because of grief."
>
> (Ps 31:6f)

Heschel points to a peril from which we increasingly suffer – our diminished image of ourselves. We do not see ourselves as God sees us. We are the produce of our experiences which for many can be overwhelming. Others seek escape routes in distractions and in distractions from distractions (Eliot).

Heschel's work 'The Prophets' appeared in 1962.[9] It is the fruit of a lifetime's work. The minds of the prophets were not religion centred. They dwelt on justice. A single act of injustice – to us might be slight, to the prophet a disaster. We continually witness acts of injustice, manifestations of hypocrisy, falsehood, outrage, misery, but we rarely get indignant about these things. To the prophets a minor, commonplace injustice assumes almost cosmic proportions.

> "Be appalled, O heavens, at this,
> be shocked, be utterly desolate, says the Lord.
> For My people have committed two evils:
> they have forsaken Me,
> the fountain of living waters
> and hewed out cisterns for themselves,
> Broken cisterns
> that can hold no water."
>
> (Jeremiah 2:12-13)

They speak and act as if the sky were to fall in because of the lack of decency. If the prophet's deep sensitivity to evil is to be called

[9] A.J. Heschel, The Prophets (New York: 1962).

hysterical, what name should be given to the deep callousness of evil which the prophet laments? "They drink wine in bowls, and anoint themselves with the finest oils; but they are not grieved over the ruin of Joseph." (Amos 6:2). Our eyes are witness to the hardness and cruelty of humankind, but our heart tries to obliterate the memories, to calm the nerves and to silence our conscience.

The prophet is one who feels fiercely. God has thrust a burden on him and he is stunned at the enormous greed and indifference of a world that can be cruel. Frightful is the agony that he sees in the heart of humankind; no human voice can convey its full terror. Prophecy is the voice that God has lent to the silent agony, a voice to the plundered poor, a voice against the profaned riches of the world. It is a form of living, a crossing point of God and man. God is raging in the prophet's words (Prophets, p. 5). God is compassion, but not a compromise, justice but not inclemency. Peace and tranquility are unknown to the prophet. The miseries and plight of the afflicted gives them no rest. Many are just hard, and callous as regards their callousness, the prophets remain examples of supreme impatience with evil. They are not distracted by power or applause, by neither success nor beauty. Their intense sensitivity to right and wrong is due to their intense sensitivity to God's concern for right and wrong. They feel and see the world with the heart and eyes of God. They sensitise us to the need for compassion and love in our world. The way we deal with envy, greed and pride points the way to how we live with God. Our negative self-image and loneliness will only begin to erode when we learn of God's care and love for us, and how he suffers when we suffer.

Yet inwardness is ignored. The Spirit has become a myth. We treat each other as if we were created in the likeness of a machine rather than in the likeness of God. All around me I see people used just because they are useful. There is no place for the sick, the elderly or the broken. We, in so many ways, have become deaf to the prophetic voice that reminds us of our dignity as children of God, created in his own image. The rabbis, in commenting on the prophets, were not guilty of exaggeration in asserting, "Whoever destroys a single soul should be considered the same as one who has destroyed a whole world. And whoever saves one single soul is to be considered the same as one who has saved a whole world." (Prophets, p. 14). Jesus' parables speak of going after the lost, of leaving the 99 sheep to find the one that is missing (Lk 15:4-7) and the other parable of mercy in Lk 15.

The prophets remind us of the moral state of the people. Few are guilty but all are responsible. An individual is in some way affected by the spirit of a society, an individual's crime discloses society's corruption. In a community not indifferent to suffering, impatient with cruelty and falsehood, continually concerned for God and all his children, crime would be infrequent rather than common. Such is not the case in our societies – including religious societies. For instance, in the modern world child-pornography and child abuse continue to grow. We are all responsible for the society that allows this.

There are always exceptions who hear the prophetic voice. For the prophet the realness of God comes first and we must find a way of living according to this reality. The Bible reveals God's view of humanity – and his dream for a renewed, healed and human society. The purpose of prophecy is to conquer callousness, to change the inner man and thus to revolutionise history (Prophets, p. 16f). This lays a burden on the prophet who feels an outsider. People prefer to hear comforting voices rather than face the reality of the situation. The prophet Jeremiah tried to teach Judah that their days were numbered and that the Babylonians were too strong. Those in Jerusalem could not accept that the Kingdom would end or that the Temple or Jerusalem could fall. They rejected Jeremiah because the old way of believing could not be wrong. Jeremiah complains:

> *"Cursed be the day*
> *On which I was born!...*
> *Because He did not kill me in the womb;*
> *So my mother would have been my grave,...*
> *Why did I come forth out of the womb*
> *To see toil and sorrow,*
> *And spend my days in shame?"*
> *Jeremiah 20:14, 17, 18*

The mission he performs is distasteful to him and repugnant to others; no reward is promised him and no reward could temper its bitterness. The prophet bears scorn and reproach (Jer. 15;15). He is stigmatised as a madman by his contemporaries, and, by some modern scholars, as abnormal.

> *They hate him who reproves in the gate,*
> *They abhor him who speaks the truth.*
>
> *Amos 5:10*

Loneliness and misery were only part of the reward that prophecy brought to Jeremiah: "I sat alone because Thy hand was upon me" (15:17). Mocked, reproached, and persecuted, he would think of casting away his task:

> *If I say, I will not mention Him,*
> *Or speak any more in His name,*
> *There is my heart as it were a burning fire*
> *Shut up in my bones,*
> *And I am weary with holding it in,*
> *And I cannot.*
>
> *Jeremiah 20:9*

Jeremiah, when chosen to become a prophet, was told by the Lord: "And I, behold, I make you this day a fortified city, an iron pillar, and bronze walls, against the whole land, against the kings of Judah, its princes, its priests, and the people of the land" (Jer. 1:18). And later he was reassured: "They will fight against you, but they shall not prevail over you" (Jer. 15:20).

The prophet is a lonely man. He alienates the wicked as well as the pious, the cynics as well as the believers, the priests and the princes, the judges and the false prophets. But to be a prophet means to challenge and to defy and to cast out fear.

The life of a prophet is not futile. People may remain deaf to a prophet's admonitions; they cannot remain callous to a prophet's existence. At the very beginning of his career, Ezekiel was told not to entertain any illusions about the effectiveness of his mission:

> *And you, son of man, be not afraid of them, nor be afraid of their words, though briers and thorns are with you and you sit upon scorpions; be not afraid of their words, nor be dismayed at their looks, ... Behold, I have made your face hard against their faces, and your forehead hard against their foreheads. Like adamant harder than flint have I made your forehead; fear them not, nor be dismayed at their looks, ... The people also are impudent and stubborn: I send you to them; and you shall say to them, Thus says the Lord God. And whether they hear or refuse to hear ... they will know that there has been a prophet among them.*
>
> *Ezekiel 2:6; 3:8-9; 2:4-5; cf. 3:27*

(Prophets, p. 18f)

Yet there is a joy in the prophet's serenade to God. Jeremiah, in spite of his laments, can still say:

> Thy words were found, and I ate them,
> Thy words became to me a joy
> The delight of my heart;
> Fir I am called by Thy name,
> O Lord, God of hosts.

(Jeremiah 15:16)

His dignity and validation comes from his relationship with God. He feels with God's heart and lives in a deep union with God. He feels deeply with God that the people do not listen.

His duty however is to warn the people not to put their trust in deceptive words. "Behold you trust in deceptive words to no avail" (Jer 7:8). Worship if it is coupled with evil acts becomes an absurdity. The Holy Place is doomed when people indulge in unholy deeds:

> "Will you steal, murder, commit adultery, swear falsely, burn incense to Baal, and go after other gods that you have not known, and then come and stand before Me in this house, which is called by My name, and say, We are delivered! – only to go on doing all these abominations? Has this house, which is called by My name, become a den of robbers in your eyes? Behold, I Myself have seen it, says the Lord. Go now to My place that was in Shiloh, where I made My name dwell at first, and see what I did to it for the wickedness of My people Israel. And now, because you have done all these things, says the Lord, and when I spoke to you persistently you did not listen, and when I called you, you did not answer, therefore I will do to the house which is called by My name, and in which you trust, and to the place which I gave to you and to your fathers, as I did to Shiloh. And I will cast you out of My sight, as I cast out all your kinsmen, all the offspring of Ephraim."
>
> (Jeremiah, 7:9-15)

The people are not to presume they are delivered. Jeremiah delivers these words at the door of the Temple. Jeremiah warns unless there is a change of heart the Temple will fall. The people think that is impossible, but Jeremiah warns the old-certainties will sustain the people no more, because the old-certainties are now disappearing.

The plight of the people causes great grief in God. He says:

> "My grief is beyond healing
> My heart is sick within me...
> For the wound of my beloved people is my heart wounded,
> I mourn, and dismay has taken hold on me.
> Is there no balm in Gilead?

Is there no physician there?
Why then has the health of my beloved people
Not been restored?
O that my head were waters,
And my eyes a fountain of tears,
That I might weep day and night
For the slain of my beloved people!...
Who will have pity on you, O Jerusalem,
Or who will bemoan You?
Who will turn aside
To ask about your welfare?"

(Jer. 8:18-9:1; 15:5)

God's heart is sick with grief. He wants to cry and cry "for the slain of my people". There is no healing from the present pain. This is what Heschel calls the "pathos" of God.

God does not repudiate his people forever. He promises a new covenant with them:

'Look, the days are coming, Yahweh declares, when I shall make a new covenant with the House of Israel (and the House of Judah), but not like the covenant I made with their ancestors the day I took them by the hand to bring them out of Egypt, a covenant which they broken even though I was their Master, Yahweh declares. No, this is the covenant I shall make with the House of Israel when those days have come, Yahweh declares. Within them I shall plant my Law, writing it on their hearts. Then I shall be their God and they will be my people. There will be no further need for everyone to teach neighbour or brother, saying, "Learn to know Yahweh!" No, they will all know me, from the least to the greatest, Yahweh declares, since I shall forgive their guilt and never more call their sin to mind.'

(Jer 31:31-34)

God will be with his people again with a new covenant written on their hearts. From the destruction and the heartache God will create anew his people (see also Ez 37; 36:34-37).

Jesus speaks in the language of the prophets. He has come to redeem humanity and show people their dignity. In the Gospel of Matthew we read:

Salt for the earth and light for the world

'You are salt for the earth. But if salt loses its taste, what can make it salty again? It is good for nothing, and can only be thrown out, to be trampled under people's feet.

'You are light for the world. A city built on a hill-top cannot be hidden. No one lights a lamp to put it under a tub; they put it on the lamp-stand where it shines for everyone in the house. In the same way, your light must shine in people's sight, so that, seeing your good works, they may give praise to your Father in heaven.'

(Mtt 5; 13-16)

We are called to be God's representatives in this world, to witness to his light and bring healing and comfort to the broken. Jesus goes on to say that he has come to fulfill the law and the prophets (Mtt 5:17-19). The purpose of the law and the prophets is to lead people into God's reign.

Rabbi Heschel, when he spoke of the death and torture, physical and psychological, of multitudes of Jews and non-Jews, points to a peril from which we increasingly suffer, namely our diminished image of ourselves. This was particularly true in his dialogue with Christians.[10] He showed through the prophets that we are a need of God and the prophets call us to become truly human as we learn compassion and soften our hearts. Jesus reminds us of our dignity. He says:

'That is why I am telling you not to worry about your life and what you are to eat, nor about your body and what you

---

[10] Edward K. Kaplan, Holiness in Words: Abraham Joshua Heschel's Poetics of Piety (New York: 1996) p. 116f.

are to wear. Surely life is more than food, and the body more than clothing! Look at the birds in the sky. They do not sow or reap or gather into barns; yet your heavenly Father feeds them. Are you not worth much more than they are? Can any of you, however much you worry, add one single cubit to your span of life? And why worry about clothing? Think of the flowers growing in the fields, they never have to work or spin; yet I assure you that not even Solomon in all his royal robes was clothed like one of these. Now if that is how God clothes the wild flowers growing in the field which are there today and thrown into the furnace tomorrow, will he not much more look after you, you who have so little faith? So do not worry; do not say, "What are we to eat? What are we to drink? What are we to wear?" It is the gentiles who set their hearts on all these things. Your heavenly Father knows you need them all. Set your hearts on his kingdom first, and on God's saving justice, and all these other things will be given you as well. So do not worry about tomorrow, tomorrow will take care of itself. Each day has enough trouble of its own.'

(Mtt 6:25-34)

Jesus uses ordinary images, birds of the air and flowers of the field to illustrate his message. This is what touched Van Gogh in his painting. Jesus teaches us that all these are treasured by God, yet each of us is more valued than any of these. We are beloved of God and precious to him and he loves us.

God identifies with the poor and broken as the prophets pointed out. Jesus teaches us this in his parable on the final judgement. He says:

'When the Son of man comes in his glory, escorted by all the angels, then he will take his seat on his throne of glory. All nations will be assembled before him and he will separate people one from another as the shepherd separates sheep from goats. He will place the sheep on his right hand and the goats on his left. Then the King will say to those on his right hand, "Come, you whom my Father has blessed, take as your heritage the kingdom prepared for you since the foundation of the world. For I was hungry and you gave me food, I was thirsty and you gave me drink, I was a stranger and you made me welcome, lacking clothes and you clothed me, sick and you visited me, in prison and you came to see me." Then the upright will say to him in reply, "Lord, when did we see you hungry and feed you, or thirsty and give you drink? When did we see you a stranger and make you welcome, lacking clothes and clothe you? When did we find you sick or in prison and go to see you?" And the King will answer, "In truth I tell you, in so far as you did this to one of the least of these brothers of mine, you did it to me." Then he will say to those on his left hand, "Go away from me, with your curse upon you, to the eternal fire prepared for the devil and his angels. For I was hungry and you never gave me food, I was thirsty and you never gave me anything to drink, I was a stranger and you never made me welcome, lacking clothes and you never clothed me, sick and in prison and you never visited me." Then it will be their turn to ask, "Lord, when did we see you hungry or thirsty, a stranger or lacking clothes, sick or in prison, and did not come to your help?" Then he will answer, "In truth I tell you, in so far as you neglected to do this to one of the least of these, you neglected to do it to me." And they will go away to eternal punishment, and the upright to eternal life.'

(Mtt 25:31-46)

When the people ask when did they see God hungry or naked, or sick, God tells them as often as you did it to the least of these you did it to me. God identifies with the broken, the sick, the hungry and those who are homeless and have no shelter. This continues what the prophets taught. In doing these things, looking after the broken, the sick etc., we become the light of the world. Sadly these people are more often rejected, but there are still those who become 'light' and make a difference.

The quest for meaning, according to Rabbi Heschel, is the quest for a relationship to that which is beyond being.[11] Biblical thought seeks to relate humanity to a transcendence called the living God. The meaning to our existence depends on whether or not we respond to God who is in search of us. Human life is also a question from God. We are constantly called to become truly human in God.

The Holy Spirit

Heschel doesn't give a theology of the Spirit, rather he shows the effects of the Spirit as the inspiration of the prophets and holy people. He mediates the Presence of God. He is as near as the throbbing of his own heart, often deep and calm but at times, overwhelming, intoxicating, setting the soul afire.[12] In his German thesis, which formed the backdrop for his later work The Prophets, there emerges a compelling confession of his own calling:

> "We understand the person impassioned with prophetic zeal, who knows himself to be in emotional agreement and harmony with God. We understand the power of Him impassioned with anger and who turns away from his people. That overwhelming knowledge [erschütterndes Wissen] of the concern and suffering that God experiences for the world, and the prophet's sharing of that lived predicament and suffering, is of such power, of such obvious value, and so unique, that even today this idea acts as a summons carrying distinct shapes and possibilities. Perhaps this is the final meaning, value, and dignity of an emotional religion. The depths of the individual soul thus become the place where the comprehension of God [Verständnis für Gott] flowers, the harmony of agreement [Einverständnis] with the transcendent pathos."[13]

---

[11] Abraham Joshua Heschel, Who is Man? (Stamford: 1965) p. 66-68.

[12] A.J. Heschel, An Analysis of Piety, The Review of Religion 6, 3 (March 1942), p. 299.

[13] A.J. Heschel, Die Prophetie (Berlin: 1933), p. 171.

For Heschel, compassion, empathy are the works of the Spirit of God, the same Spirit who inspires the prophets.

Heschel's next major work was on the Jewish thinker Maimonides. He speaks of Maimonides' search to know God. It is God by his Spirit who inspires this search:

> "His thought, his reflections, his concentration on that problem determined his spiritual attitude for his entire life. His passion of the intellect, his almost naive desire to understand, his quest and his research to achieve an understanding of that secret never ended; for in his mind, which ceaselessly throbbed with emotion, the longing for God came not only from a vague, dark feeling, but more from an intellectual necessity: that yearning thought is what provoked his research into a metaphysical system."[14]

He sees the Kabbalah as being inspired by God's Spirit. He speaks of the inspiration of holy men in the following way:

> "One cannot grasp the innermost thought of the holy men of Israel without remembering that in their eyes, prophetic inspiration hovered over human reason, and, at times, heaven and earth would meet and kiss. They believed that the divine voice that issued from Horeb was not stilled thereafter. "These commandments the Lord spoke in a great voice to your whole assembly on the mountain out of the fire, the cloud and the thick mist, then he said no more" (Deuteronomy 5:19). Onkelos translated (and also Targum Jonathan), "it – the great voice – has not ceased from speaking." [note 196: Rashi adds: "for His voice is mighty and exists forever." This interpretation is found also in the Babylonian Talmud, Sanhedrin 17b and Sotah 10b.]"[15]

---

[14] A.J. Heschel, Maimonides: A Biography (New York: 1982), p. 157.

[15] Edward K. Kaplan, op. cit, p. 139.

In his work 'God in Search of Man' he explains that the divine encounter is still possible. God inspires the actions of a holy man by the Spirit (see 'Man is Not Alone', p. 67-79). We are led into the Presence of God. "Our awareness of God is a syntax of his silence in which our souls mingle with the divine, in which the ineffable in us communes with the ineffable beyond us" (Man is Not Alone, p. 74). He is not a being, but being in and beyond all things (Man is Not Alone, p. 78).

In God in Search of Man he says:

> For God is not always silent, and man is not always blind. His glory fills the world; His spirit hovers above the waters. There are moments in which, to use a Talmudic phrase, heaven and earth kiss each other; in which there is a lifting of the veil at the horizon of the known, opening a vision of what is eternal in time. Some of us have at least caught a glimpse of the beauty, peace, and power that flow through the souls of those who are devoted to Him. There may come a moment like a thunder in the soul, when man is not only aided, not only guided by God's mysterious hand, but also taught how to aid, how to guide other beings. The voice of Sinai goes on forever: "These words the Lord spoke unto all your assembly in the mount out of the midst of the fire, of the cloud, and of the thick darkness, with *a great voice that goes on for ever*" [Heschel's emphasis].
>
> (God in Search of Man, p. 138)

The Spirit can use loneliness, despair and desperation to unlock the human mind and spirit. He says:

> Only those who have gone through days on which words were of no avail, on which the most brilliant theories jarred the ear like mere slang; only those who have experienced ultimate not-knowing, the voicelessness of a soul struck by wonder, total muteness, are able to enter the meaning of God, a meaning greater than the mind.

There is a loneliness in us that hears. When the soul parts from the company of the ego and its retinue of petty conceits; when we cease to exploit all things but instead pray the world's cry, the world's sigh, our loneliness may hear the living grace beyond all power.

(Man is Not Alone, p. 140f)

Our loneliness is where we meet God. By his Spirit he is present to us demonstrating that alienation is not final. He goes on to say "All those who bring beauty, art and hope are manifestations for us of the Spirit."

"We must first peer into the darkness, feel strangled and entombed in the hopelessness of living without God, before we are ready to feel the presence of His living light.
"And it shall come to pass, when I bring a cloud over the earth, that the bow shall be seen in the cloud" (Genesis 9:14). When ignorance and confusion blot out all thoughts, the light of God may suddenly burst forth in the mind like a rainbow in the sky. Our understanding of the greatness of God comes about as an act of illumination. As the Baal Shem said, "like a lightning that all of a sudden illumines the world, God illumines the mind of man, enabling him to understand the greatness of our Creator." This is what is meant by the words of the Psalmist: "He sent out His arrows and scattered [the clouds]; He shot forth lightnings and discomfited them." The darkness retreats, "The channels of water appeared, the foundations of the world were laid bare." (Psalms 18:15-16)

God's Spirit is ever active. Heschel's testimony helps us accept in our humanity loneliness and alienation, but when accepted in the worship of God we allow his Spirit to work. No matter how deep the night we are close to God who brings us to new life.

For Heschel there is meaning beyond absurdity and every deed and word matter. We must hold our life as if it were a work of art. Prayer begins at the edge of emptiness, when our power ends. He believes that wonder rather than doubt is the root of all knowledge. The signs of the Spirit are everywhere. 'All is Grace' says Thérèse of Lisieux.

Becoming Human:

Thérèse of Lisieux became totally herself in giving herself (abandon) to God. She came to know Jesus and gave herself in his Spirit to the Father. In the Christian dispensation the work of the Spirit is closely related to the work of Jesus.

Paul uses the term "in Christ" (*en Christo*).[16] He means to be understood as having an experience of the risen and living Christ. In Philippians 1:13f he says: "My chains in Christ have become known to all the praetorium, but to everybody else and most of the brothers in the Lord have gained confidence from my chains…" In Phil 2:1f he says: "So if in Christ there is anything that will move you, any incentive in love, any fellowship in the Spirit, any warmth or sympathy – I appeal to you make my joy complete by being of a single mind, one in love, one in heart and mind." He speaks of his hope for the future 'in the Lord' (2:19, 24) and his assurance of divine enabling (4:13). He does not hesitate to make an emotive appeal to refresh his heart (*splanchna*) in Christ or to express his deep longings "in the deep feelings (*splanchnois*) of Christ" (Phm 1:20; Phil 1:8 and 2:1). 'Splanchna' in Greek means the inner part, the seat of emotions. Paul felt himself to be caught up "in Christ" and borne along by the Spirit. In Christ (*en Christo*) and in the Spirit (*en pneumati*) are used interchangeably by Paul. In Gal 2:19-20 Paul says "I have been crucified with Christ, and it is no longer I that live but Christ lives in me".

In Colossians 1:27f Paul says: "It was God's purpose to reveal to them how rich is the glory of this mystery among the gentiles: it is Christ among you, your hope of glory, this is the Christ we are proclaiming, admonishing and instructing everyone in all wisdom to make everyone perfect in Christ." In Ephesians we have the prayer "… so that Christ

[16] See A. Oepke, en, TDNT, p. 538.

may live in your hearts through faith and then planted in love and built on love ... so that knowing the love of Christ, which is beyond knowledge, you will be filled with the utter fullness of God" (Eph 3:17-20). In Christ we become a new creation. "So for everyone who is in Christ there is a new creation: the old order is gone and a new being is there to see" (2 Cor 5:17). From the salvation of the individual God hopes to save all and create a new heaven and a new earth (Rev 21:1f).

In Von Balthasar's Theodrama (vol 3) he sees Jesus becoming the person he was called to be in living out the mission of the Father. He says that the "authentic, primal archetype or idea of every human begin is the incarnate, crucified and risen Son, who is the final idea of God, mediating all creation" quoting Maximus the Confessor (TD3, 258). In his Son, the Word, he sees all of Jesus' brothers and sisters.

God sends his Spirit so that we can learn what mission God calls us to in Christ. In this way we become the people we are called to be. We are incorporated in the person of Christ in God's theodrama of salvation (TD3, p. 203). Person is the new name by which God addresses me (Rev 2:17).

In Christ (*en Christo*) (TD3, 241) we are given a share in God's salvific work in Jesus for the world. We are called to share his suffering. The completion of "what is lacking in Christ's affliction for the sake of the body, that is the Church" (Col 1:24) takes place in faith, but can also be experienced by those with certain mystical gifts. Here Von Balthasar has in mind Adrienne Von Speyr. Thérèse of Lisieux experienced a deep night of faith in the last eighteen months of her life. In faith and darkness she shared Jesus' work for the salvation of the world. She did not have the assurance of Von Speyr.

Chapter 5

Winter Light

Ingmar Bergman (+2007) was a Swedish film director, writer and producer. One of his most famous films was The Seventh Seal (1957). In 1963 he made a film which he said was among his favourites – 'Winter Light'. As a young man he lost his faith and in making this film he came to peace with his decision. On a cold winter's Sunday, the pastor of a small rural church performs services for a tiny congregation, though he is tormented by a severe crisis of faith. After the service he attempts to console a fisherman (Jonas) who is tormented by anxiety, but Tomas, the pastor, can only think of his own troubled relationship with God. A school teacher, Marta, offers her love to Tomas but he is conflicted and confused. This film is the second in a trilogy of films made by Bergman dealing with man's relationship with God.

The first film in the series was 'Through a Glass Darkly' (1961) and the final film was 'The Silence' (1963). Bergman called the trilogy 'The Silence of God'. His works dealt with loss of faith, loneliness, bleakness and insanity. He influenced people like Michelangelo Antonioni (+2007) who preferred his audience to contemplate his movies. He showed through metaphor and allusion the emptiness of modern life. He reflects for us the loneliness of our world.

Holy Mother:

In a benefit concert for Bosnia in 1996 Eric Clapton performed the song he wrote for the Blessed Mother, and joined with the great Italian opera singer Luciano Pavarotti and a wonderful Gospel choir. The words of the song are a genuine prayer to Mary from Clapton. The song expresses a rise from despair to hope, and forth, from loneliness to reconciliation with himself and with God. The concert footage showed a host of fans Clapton's spiritual side.

The song goes back to the 1980s. In his memoir "Clapton: The Autobiography"[1] the musician writes about a rock bottom moment he had in his life. He says:

> "I was in complete despair, in the privacy of my room, I begged for help. I had no notion who I thought I was talking to, I just knew that I had come to the end of my tether . . . and, going down on my knees, I surrendered. Within a few days I realised that . . . I had found a place to turn to, a place I'd always known was there but never really wanted, or needed, to believe in. From that day until this, I have never failed to pray in the morning, on my knees, asking for help, and at night, to express gratitude for my life and, most of all, for my sobriety."

He wrote Holy Mother before his final surrender in the rehab centre, when he was beset with depression and self-loathing. After seeing Prince in concert he felt his courage come back somewhat and penned 'Holy Mother'. His life was at a low ebb, he cried out and sensed that the Holy Mother was there and he found courage to face despair and begin to heal.

Holy Mother, where are you?
Tonight I feel broken in two.
I've seen the stars fall from the sky.
Holy mother, can't keep from crying.

Oh I need your help this time,
Get me through this lonely night.
Tell me please which way to turn
To find myself again.

Holy mother, hear my prayer,
Somehow I know you're still there.
Send me please some peace of mind;
Take away this pain.

I can't wait, I can't wait, I can't wait any longer.
I can't wait, I can't wait, I can't wait for you.

[1] E. Clapton, Clapton: The Autobiography (New York: 2008).

Holy mother, hear my cry,
I've cursed your name a thousand times.
I've felt the anger running through my soul;
All I need is a hand to hold.

Oh I feel the end has come,
No longer my legs will run.
You know I would rather be
In your arms tonight.

When my hands no longer play,
My voice is still, I fade away.
Holy mother, then I'll be
Lying in, safe within your arms.

In the 1960s when Clapton was famous there were counterculture enthusiasts who wrote on subway walls "Clapton is God". Stardom and the rock-lifestyle took over yet Clapton always had an awareness of God but always took the wrong choices in life. His life was in a downward spiral of drink and drugs when he made his surrender to God and found peace. One time when he felt at his lowest and prayed for help, he felt a holy maternal presence and he wrote 'Holy Mother'. When he calls to Holy Mother he feels broken and he can't keep the tears away. He needs help to get through the lonely night. He senses Mary is near but he complains he can't wait. The end of the song is an act of faith that he will be safe in her arms. "Pray for us sinners now and at the hour of our death. Amen."

Charles Péguy (+1914) was a French essayist and poet who for a while lost his faith but one day he announced to a friend he had returned to the faith. The figure of Mary gently led him to her son Jesus. He wrote a poem entitled "The Portal of the Mystery of Hope" (Le Porche du Mystère de la Deuxième Vertu). He speaks of how God himself is surprised by hope:

But hope, says God, that is something that surprises me.
Even me.
That is surprising.
That these poor children see how things are going and believe that tomorrow things will go better.
That they see how things are going today and believe that they

will go better tomorrow morning.
That is surprising and it's by far the greatest marvel of our
grace.
And I'm surprised by it myself.
And my grace must indeed be an incredible force,
And must flow freely and like an inexhaustible river.
Since the first time it flowed and since it has forever been
flowing.
In my natural and supernatural creation.
In my spiritual and carnal and yet spiritual creation.
In my eternal and temporal and yet eternal creation.
Mortal and immortal.

There is so much that militates against hope in our world – yet in the midst of despair there often comes someone who re-ignites our hope – it can be a saint, a poet, or maybe an artist. I think of the effect of listening to the song The Rose where love seems lost yet in the spring blooms again. Hope against hope is a great miracle.

What surprises me, says God, is hope.
And I can't get over it.
This little hope who seems like nothing at all.
This little girl hope.
Immortal.

Because my three virtues, says God.
The three virtues, my creatures.
My daughters, my children.
Are themselves like my other creatures.
Of the race of men.
Faith is a loyal Wife.
Charity is a Mother.
An ardent mother, noble-hearted.
Or an older sister who is like a mother.
Hope is a little girl, nothing at all.
Who came into the world on Christmas day just this past year.

Jesus came as a defenseless child who was rejected and died. He is the face in Roualt's painting, infinitely sad. He is the Jesus of Pascal whose suffering continues in the sufferings of every person until the end of time. Their tears "are the tears of the child" who hopes because God's love is more powerful than death and leads us through death to new life.

The central mystery of Christianity is the incarnation. According to the traditional adage of the Fathers of the Church, God truly became man so that we could truly become God. All mistrust of the flesh, all hatred of the temporal, is therefore an abomination, for it is a mistrust and hatred of the very real conditions that the Word has assumed in order to redeem them. God so loved the world – and not only souls, but bodies, the earth, creation – that he sent his only Son.

One creature is the prototype of the new humanity redeemed by Christ: Mary, the mother of Jesus. She is superior both to humans and to angels, because while she is carnal like humans, she is also pure like the angels, without the shadow of sin. She alone is a perfect imitation of Jesus, because she alone is wholly terrestrial and wholly divinised. Péguy's devotion to Mary, far from being an overly devout pietism, is an exultation of the temporal by the eternal, and a glorification of the flesh by the spirit.

In the poem Péguy speaks of the woodcutter who brings his sick children to Mary, because she is the unique intercessor. She is "hope" itself. This is autobiographical in that Péguy is here referring to himself.

> His three children in sickness, in the misery where they lay.
> And he had peacefully given them to you.
> In prayer he had given them to you.
> Placed very peacefully within the arms of she who bears all of
> the world's sufferings.
> And whose arms are already so full.
> Because the Son has taken all sin upon himself
> The mother has taken all sorrow.

Péguy's picture of Mary is influenced by St. John's picture of her at the foot of the Cross of her son. There she stands with the beloved disciple (Jn 19:25-27). Jesus breathes out his Spirit on this community and they become his Spirit bearers to the world. Mary sees the death of her son and now she shares the tears of all Jesus' brothers and sisters, whose mother she has become, too. Her son took away all sins, she bears all our tears.

So then the 'woodcutter' takes his courage in his hands and presents the sick ones to Mary, to "she who intercedes".

And so you must gather your courage with both hands.
And address yourself directly to she who is above them all.
Be bold. Just once. Address yourself boldly to she who is infinitely beautiful.
Because she's also infinitely good.

To she who intercedes.
The only one who can speak with the authority of a mother.
Address yourself boldly to she who is infinitely pure.
Because she's also infinitely gentle.

To she who is infinitely noble.
Because she's also infinitely gracious.
Infinitely courteous.
Courteous like the priest who at the threshold of the church goes to meet the newborn at the threshold.
On the day of his baptism.
To introduce him into the house of God.

To she who is infinitely rich.
Because she's also infinitely poor.
To she who is infinitely lofty.
Because she's also infinitely lowly.

To she who is infinitely great.
Because she's also infinitely small.
Infinitely humble.
A young mother.

To she who is infinitely righteous.
Because she's also infinitely yielding.

To she who is infinitely joyful.
Because she's also infinitely sorrowful.

This page is autobiographical because as he admitted privately his devotion to Mary enabled him to return to a deeper faith and new hope. Our tears are God's. Mary shows us the maternal love of God. As St. Maximilian Kolbe says "the Holy Spirit is the Immaculate Conception" and Mary is uniquely united with God's Holy Spirit. In this Spirit she is one with the tears of humanity praying all the time that those tears be transformed and we find our home in the New Jerusalem where every tear will be wiped away.

Péguy goes on to develop his theme of hope. Mary has led him to God. Now he reflects on the hope of God. He tells us:

> You must have confidence in God, he certainly has had confidence in us.
> You must trust God, he certainly has put his trust in us.
> You must hope in God, he has certainly hoped in us.
> You must give God a chance, he has certainly given us a chance.
> What chance.
> Every chance.
> You must have faith in God, he certainly has faith in us.

God sees the good in each of us. He knows there is sinfulness but he has come that we might die to sinfulness. He has come that we might have life and have it to the full (Jn 10:10). Péguy shows the faith and hope God has in us. He repeats:

> It's God who gave us a chance, who put his trust in us.
> Who gave us credence, who had faith in us.
> Will this confidence be misplaced, will it be said that this confidence was misplaced.
> God put his hope in us. He took the initiative. He hoped that the least of the sinners,
> That the tiniest of the sinners would at least work a little for his own salvation.
> Just a little, as poorly as it might be.
> That he would look after it a bit.
> He hoped in us, will it be said that we didn't hope in him.
> God placed his hope, his poor hope in each one of us, in the tiniest of the sinners. Will it be said that we tiny ones, that we sinners will it be we who do not place our hope in him.

Péguy complained that we do not know or hear the word of God. He tries in his poetry to open our eyes and ears to the love that is around us and there to see the love of God revealed in the Word made flesh (Jn 1:14). The Word of God is ultimately a word of love for each of us.

> The word of God is not a tangled ball of yarn.
> It's a beautiful woolen thread which winds itself around the spindle.
> As he spoke too us, thus we ought to listen.
> As he spoke to Moses.
> As he spoke to us through Jesus.
> As he spoke to us all, thus we ought to listen.
>
> Yes, my child, if that's how it is, if it's like this that we ought to listen to Jesus.
> That we ought to listen to God.

Jesus Participates in Our Loneliness:

The letter to the Hebrews is written to a group of Hebrew Christians. The worship of the old-covenant has been superseded by the sacrifice of Jesus Christ. The group are encouraged not to abandon the Christian faith (e.g. 2:1-3; 3:12; 6:4-6). In a time of discouragement he points them to Jesus the new high-priest of the new covenant. The author begins:

> At many moments in the past and by many means, God spoke to our ancestors through the prophets; but in our time, the final days, he has spoken to us in the person of his Son, whom he appointed heir of all things and through whom he made the ages. He is the reflection of God's glory and bears the impress of God's own being, sustaining all things by his powerful command; and now that he has purged sins away, he has taken his seat at the right hand of the divine Majesty on high. So he is now as far above the angels as the title which he has inherited is higher than their own name.
>
> (Heb 1:1-4)

In the old dispensation God spoke to the fathers of the Hebrews through the prophets and other means. Now he speaks through Jesus, his Son. He is the reflection of the Father's glory. Apaugasma (here translated reflection) can be understood as radiance, or reflection, refulgence. He bears the very impress of God's being. This recalls Wisdom 7:26. Here the author speaks of Wisdom as "… a reflection of the eternal light, untarnished mirror of God's active power and the image of his goodness".

Thus Jesus suffered, died and rose again to be enthroned at God's right hand.

> "Since all the children share the same human nature, he too shared equally in it, so that by his death he could set aside him who held the power of death, namely the devil, and set free all those who had been held in slavery all their lives by the fear of death. For it was not the angels that he took to himself; he took to himself the line of Abraham. It was essential that he should in this way be made completely like his brothers so that he could become a compassionate and trustworthy high priest for their relationship to God, able to expiate the sins of the people. For the suffering he himself passed through while being put to the test enables him to help others when they are being put to the test. (Heb 2:14-18)

Jesus by his death destroyed death, the last enemy (1 Cor 15:26). Jesus became like all his brothers and sisters. This is how Jesus became a faithful high priest. Being faithful is something the perfect high priest is expected to be. This goes back to Samuel in 1 Sam 2:35. He is also merciful because he has suffered as all human beings do. This motif is taken up again in 4:15 and 5:1-3 and explains Jesus' solidarity with human beings. The temptations Jesus suffered were not only the temptations at the passion, but those experienced throughout his life (see 4:15; Lk 22:28). Jesus is the merciful and faithful high priest whose priesthood lasts forever. Here we recall Ps 110:4, "You are a priest forever, a priest like Melchizedek of old". This is reiterated in 4:14-5:10:

> Since in Jesus, the Son of God, we have the supreme high priest who has gone through to the highest heaven, we must hold firm to our profession of faith. For the high priest we

have is not incapable of feeling our weaknesses with us, but has been put to the test in exactly the same way as ourselves, apart from sin. Let us, then, have no fear in approaching the throne of grace to receive mercy and to find grace when we are in need of help.

Every high priest is taken from among human beings and is appointed to act on their behalf in relationships with God, to offer gifts and sacrifices for sins; he can sympathise with those who are ignorant or who have gone astray, because he too is subject to the limitations of weakness. That is why he has to make sin offerings for himself as well as for the people. No one takes this honour on himself; it needs a call from God, as in Aaron's case. And so it was not Christ who gave himself the glory of becoming high priest, but the one who said to him: You are my Son, today I have fathered you, and in another text: You are a priest for ever, of the order of Melchizedek. During his life on earth, he offered up prayer and entreaty, with loud cries and tears, to the one who had the power to save him from death, and, winning a hearing by his reverence, he learnt obedience, Son though he was, through his sufferings; when he had been perfected, he became for all who obey him the source of eternal salvation and was acclaimed by God with the title of high priest of the order of Melchizedek.

(Heb 4:14-5:10)

These verses recall 2:16-3:1. The author points out that Jesus, the high priest, was tempted but did not succumb to them. We can have confident access to God through the prayer of Jesus. He can pray for services because he can sympathise with those who suffer and struggle. As Paul says: "He died on the cross through weakness, but now he lives through the power of God" (2 Cor 13:4). In the days of his flesh contains a reference to Jesus' experience in Gethsemane (Mk 14:32-42) where "his soul was sorrowful even unto death" (Mk 14:34). Yet he abandoned himself to God's will. Jesus' priesthood is contrasted in 7:23-24 with the Levitical priesthood. Now Jesus' priesthood is above that since he learnt "obedience through suffering". Now his priesthood is eternal and we are saved in him. In 12:2 the author encourages us: "Let us keep our eyes fixed on Jesus who leads us in our faith and brings it to perfection: for the sake of the joy which lay before him, he endured the cross, disregarding the shame of it and has taken his seat at the right of God's throne". In the Gospel of John we read the account of the death of Jesus:

> Near the cross of Jesus stood his mother and his mother's sister, Mary the wife of Clopas, and Mary of Magdala. Seeing his mother and the disciple whom he loved standing near her, Jesus said to his mother, 'Woman, this is your son.' Then to the disciple he said, 'This is your mother.' And from that hour the disciple took her into his home.
> After this, Jesus knew that everything had now been completed and, so that the scripture should be completely fulfilled, he said:
> I am thirsty.
> A jar full of sour wine stood there; so, putting a sponge soaked in the wine on a hyssop stick, they held it up to his mouth. After Jesus had taken the wine he said, 'It is fulfilled'; and bowing his head he gave up his spirit.
>
> (Jn 19:25-29)

At the Cross the "beloved disciple" and Mary, "mother" become a new family. The beloved disciple is not named because he stands for all disciples who stand at the foot of the cross. Mary is not named; she is called "mother". Eve was called Mother of the living (see Gen 3:20); now Mary is Mother of the living in the new community. Jesus cries "I thirst". Thérèse of Lisieux saw this as a thirst for love. Then he cries "it is accomplished" (tetelestai). He has now made a new community that will keep his spirit alive and ultimately become a new creation, bringing in the new heaven and the new earth (Rev 21-22). Then Jesus hands over his spirit (paradoken) and dies.

Yet love is stronger than death. On the Sunday the women find the tomb empty. The beloved disciple comes to behold that Jesus is alive. Jesus meets Mary of Magdala:

> But Mary was standing outside near the tomb, weeping. Then, as she wept, she stooped to look inside, and saw two angels in white sitting where the body of Jesus had been, one at the head, the other at the feet. They said, 'Woman, why are you weeping?' 'They have taken my Lord away,' she replied, 'and

I don't know where they have put him.' As she said this she turned round and saw Jesus standing there, though she did not realise that it was Jesus. Jesus said to her, 'Woman, why are you weeping? Who are you looking for?' Supposing him to be the gardener, she said, 'Sir, if you have taken him away, tell me where you have put him, and I will go and remove him.' Jesus said, 'Mary!' She turned round then and said to him in Hebrew, 'Rabbuni!' – which means Master. Jesus said to her, 'Do not cling to me, because I have not yet ascended to the Father. But go to the brothers, and tell them: 'I am ascending to my Father and your Father, to my God and your God.' So Mary of Magdala told the disciples, 'I have seen the Lord,' and that he had said these things to her.

(Jn 20:11-18)

His return (Jn 14:18-19; 16:23) is his exaltation to the right hand of the Father. Jesus is now alive and filled with the Holy Spirit. He is now glorified and this is why he tells Mary not to touch him. Initially Mary mistook Jesus for the gardener. She did not suspect there was such a thing as resurrection, but when Jesus addressed her personally she knew it was truly him.

Next Jesus appears to the terrified apostles:

In the evening of that same day, the first day of the week, the doors were closed in the room where the disciples were, for fear of the Jews. Jesus came and stood among them. He said to them, 'Peace be with you,' and, after saying this, he showed them his hands and his side. The disciples were filled with joy at seeing the Lord, and he said to them again, 'Peace be with you.
'As the Father sent me,
so am I sending you.'
After saying this he breathed on them and said:
Receive the Holy Spirit.
If you forgive anyone's sins,
they are forgiven;
if you retain anyone's sins,
they are retained.

Thomas, called the Twin, who was one of the Twelve, was not with them when Jesus came. So the other disciples said to him, 'We have seen the Lord,' but he answered, 'Unless I can see the holes that the nails made in his hands and can put my finger into the holes they made, and unless I can put my hand into his side, I refuse to believe.' Eight days later the disciples were in the house again and Thomas was with them. The doors were closed, but Jesus came in and stood among them. 'Peace be with you,' he said. Then he spoke to Thomas, 'Put your finger here; look, here are my hands. Give me your hand; put it into my side. Do not be unbelieving any more but believe.' Thomas replied, 'My Lord and my God!' Jesus said to him:
You believe because you can see me.
Blessed are those who have not seen
and yet believe.'   (Jn 20:19-29)

Peace was one of the promised gifts of Jesus (Jn 14:27). Now that he is glorified, he pours out his spirit on them – Jesus is now no longer constrained to the limits of our space-time continuum. He can appear and disappear. He is filled with the Holy Spirit and lives forever. The Spirit accomplishes God's indwelling (Jn 14:17) and flows from the exalted Jesus as a source of eternal life (Jn 7:39). The disciples now have the power to forgive in Jesus' name.

Last of all the Lord appears to Thomas. He has refused to believe. How can such a thing be? Jesus appears and asks him to touch the places where he was wounded. Thomas exclaims "My Lord and my God" – from doubting he has come to make a supreme act of faith (Jn 20:28). All these were written so that we might have faith. By entering the drama of the Gospel we can hear the words of Jesus addressed to us today. This is the genius of the saints. In contemplating the Gospel we can meet Jesus who is alive and filled with the Holy Spirit. We too can hear his words and experience his love.

The Courage to Accept Acceptance

Paul Tillich (+1968) was a German theologian. He served as a chaplain during the First World War. He had a nervous breakdown due to his experiences. In his recovery he was helped by his love of art and beauty. This helped restore his broken spirits. Like others (e.g. Bultmann) he saw that the words used in teaching faith and giving consolation to the dying and the wounded were weak – we had not yet a language to communicate the consolation of the faith. His life's aim as a theologian was to find a language that could help communicate the message of God in Jesus and bring his "peace" to troubled souls. He was forced to leave Germany when Hitler came to power and live and work in the United States.

Tillich sees the Cross as God's ultimate revelation. It is definitive and unsurpassable. In this act Jesus denies himself but doesn't lose himself. Only one who is united with the ground of being without separation. In resigning all claims to ultimacy and power Jesus becomes "completely transformed to the mystery he reveals.[2] Revelation comes to mean the answer to our human needs: the need to escape from our situation of estrangement, of alienation, of separation from others, of the meaninglessness of so much in life, the irrationality of the world around us, the nihilism of violence, which human beings use against each other. Only the presence of the living God in our midst, in an alienated world and in our alienation, can penetrate this darkness, bring our estrangement to an end and reconcile as the ground of being, God who helps us become creative, gives us meaning and gives us hope. The Cross shows the presence of God in our midst and shows us God is part of a broken world. Yet he overcame this brokenness and leads us to new life in the Spirit.

God himself participates without reserve in human existence. The Cross shows he participates totally in our estrangement and alienation, suffering and death. By entering into loneliness he brings it to an end. He makes this loneliness his own and experiences the deepest loneliness the world has known. He overcomes this with love. Love proves stronger than death and he rises again to new life. Jesus involves the Father in what he does. On the Cross God takes the estrangement, the meaninglessness, and the despair of human of human existence into himself. He allows himself become vulnerable to the ultimate negatives of life. When God takes death into himself, it does not mean the end of God but the end of death. God is with Jesus in all these trials, even though for a while Jesus experiences God as absent as the time when the two are most united in the Spirit. God

[2] P. Tillich, Systematic Theology, Vol 1 (Chicago: 1951) p. 133.

reconciles us, not by pretending that we are not estranged, but by being present to us where, when and how we exist. Those parts of us that are broken are now being transformed by Jesus who lives and by the power of the Spirit who is present to us in our brokenness. The man on the Cross is a realisation in history of the eternal message that nothing in heaven or earth can separate us from the love of God revealed in Jesus.

Real love consists in sharing the reality of another, and in Jesus, God has participated in our human reality. In Jesus Christ, God's acceptance and love of us has reached into our lives in all its aspects, God has participated in the negatives of human existence because he loves us, accepts us as we are and in love helps to transform us from within (Systematic Theology 1, p. 270). On the Cross he forgives and claims us because in accepting us he wants to remove anything that would keep us from a communion of love with him. Reconciliation is the removal of all barriers that block our vision of God. Tillich calls this love, agape. This is the love of God that accepts, invites us to him in Christ by the power of the Holy Spirit and transforms us into people of love and creativity – the Cross is the expression and revelation of this love. Since it is an event in God it is the source of the message "which is at the very heart of Christianity and makes possible the courage to affirm faith in Christ, namely that in spite of all the forces of separation between God and man, that is overcome from the side of God."[3]

God reaches out to us in loving acceptance from the cross. The Eucharist is a revelatory event where we participate in the mystery (e.g. see 1 Cor 11:17-33). In the first letter of Saint John we read God is love (1 Jn 4:8,16) and in the letter to the Colossians we read of Jesus that "he is the image of the unseen God, the first born of all creation..." (Col 1:13) and in Christ "lives the fullness of the divinity" (Co 2:9).

In Tillich's work "The Courage to Be"[4] he defines faith as the courage to accept acceptance. God is love (1 Jn 4:8,16) and accepts us yet we are often blinded from this by our own experiences. God is perfect love yet we do not really experience perfect love in this life. Very often we can suffer from a negation of love which occurs in abuse and rejection. This can render us afraid of love because we do not believe deep down that we are worthy or

[3] Paul Tillich, The Dynamics of Faith (New York: 1958) p. 104.

[4] P. Tillich, The Courage to Be (Chicago: 1952).

that the lines of Scripture apply to us. That is why Tillich says it takes courage to go beyond ourselves and surrender to that perfect love and acceptance that is in God.

Paul the Apostle when he felt bold and brash had no problem in accepting acceptance, but in the second letter to the Corinthians he has to come to a new reality, a new form of acceptance. In Corinth a new group had come full of confidence and boastfulness, a group Paul calls sarcastically "superapostles". They are leading the people astray (2 Cor 11-12) preaching a "different Christ". Paul's experience can speak to many people's experience. In all walks of life (including the religious) people come forward who believe they are the ones "in the know" and see themselves as being the ones who really know. However they do not know as much as they think. With great ignorance comes great confidence.

Paul retorts that he can boast too, and then proceeds to do so (2 Cor 11:21-29). However he now proceeds to make a new argument. He speaks of his own weakness:

> I am boasting because I have to. Not that it does any good, but I will move on to visions and revelations from the Lord. I know a man in Christ who fourteen years ago – still in the body? I do not know; or out of the body? I do not know: God knows – was caught up right into the third heaven. And I know that this man – still in the body, or outside the body? I do not know, God knows – was caught up into Paradise and heard words said that cannot and may not be spoken by any human being. On behalf of someone like that I am willing to boast, but I am not going to boast on my own behalf except of my weaknesses; and then, if I do choose to boast I shall not be talking like a fool because I shall be speaking the truth. But I will not go on in case anybody should rate me higher than he sees and hears me to be, because of the exceptional greatness of the revelations.
> Wherefore, so that I should not get above myself, I was given a thorn in the flesh, a messenger from Satan to batter me and prevent me from getting above myself. About this, I have three times pleaded with the Lord that it might leave me; but he has

answered me, 'My grace is enough for you: for power is at full stretch in weakness.' It is, then, about my weaknesses that I am happiest of all to boast, so that the power of Christ may rest upon me; and that is why I am glad of weaknesses, insults, constraints, persecutions and distress for Christ's sake. For it is when I am weak that I am strong.

(2 Cor 12:1-10)

Paul here speaks of his own visions and knowing a man who was caught up into the third heaven. This is Paul himself. However he was given a "thorn in the flesh". This was either a psychic or physical ailment, which in Jewish tradition was caused by a demon or Satan.[5] Paul now had an experience of weakness and he prayed fervently to be relieved of this weakness but he was told, "My grace is enough for you. My power is made perfect in weakness". It is God who is in charge. Paul has to come to accept he is weak but he is accepted as he is and he has to learn to accept himself as he is. When he was strong this was not a problem, but now he has to learn all over again. God is at work even in Paul's weakness and accepts Paul as he is.

Paul began the letter: "Blessed be the God and Father of our Lord Jesus Christ, the merciful Father and the God who gives every possible encouragement, he supports us in every hardship, so that we are able to come to the help of others, using the same kind of help we have received from God." (2 Cor 1:3f). When Eric Clapton made his recovery he continued to work to help others, founding the Crossroads Centre for drug and alcohol addiction in Antigua (1998). These are two half-way houses in Antigua for people recovering and since 1999 Clapton has organised the Crossroads Guitar Festival at Madison Square Garden to help fund the Crossroads Centre. Those who have helped out are people like B.B. King, Keith Richards and Jeff Beck. These festivals are to generate funds for the Crossroads' experience. The fifth one took place in 2013. Clapton is passing on what he himself received.

---

[5] see K. L. Schmidt, TDNT3, p. 819.

Chapter 6

Wrapped in Love

The 'Christ of St. John of the Cross' is a painting by Salvador Dalí in 1951: It depicts Jesus Christ on the cross in a darkened sky floating over a body of water complete with a boat and fishermen. The early apostles were fishermen. The figure of Jesus is devoid of nails, blood and a crown of thorns. Dalí explained his inspiration: "in the first place, in 1950, I had a 'cosmic dream' in which I saw this image in colour and which in my dream represented the 'nucleus of the atom'. The nucleus later took on a metaphysical state. I considered it the very centre of the universe, the Christ."[1] The design used by Dalí is based on a drawing by the 16th century Carmelite friar, John of the Cross. I remember visiting this painting in Glasgow and finding myself struck by its size and beauty. This piece of art enraptured me. Von Balthasar[2] spoke of this enrapturing as an analogy to the way God's love expresses itself and enraptures us. Dalí's painting shows Christ suspended without nails. He was painting his dream in the manner of the surrealists of which Dalí was a part. His vision of the 'nucleus' made him think of Christ as the centre of the world. He overlooks the ordinary lives of the people. He is the image of the invisible God (Col. 1:29) and he holds the world in love.

In John of the Cross's 'Canticle' he speaks of the eyes of God looking in love on the soul: "It seems to her that he is now always gazing upon her" (CA 11:4). When we see the look of love we are "enlightened".[3] We are enlightened when we are loved. The Gospels and the sacred writings are God's 'gaze of love'. They mediate God's love. "For God, to gaze is to love and to work favours (CB 19:6). God's gaze works four blessings in the soul. It cleanses the person, makes her beautiful, enriches and enlightens her"

[1] Robert Descharnes, Dalí (New York: 2003).

[2] Hans Urs Von Balthasar, Love Alone is Credible (San Francisco: 1982).

[3] see Kieran Kavanagh and Otilio Rodriguez, The Complete Works of St. John of the Cross (ICS: 1991). LF = Living Flame of Love; N = Dark Night of the Soul; A = Ascent of Mount Carmel; CA = Spiritual Canticle (version A); CB = Spiritual Canticle (version B); LB = Living Flame (version B).

(CB 33:1). Our lives are the effects of God who constantly gazes on us in love, and elicits beauty in us:

> "You looked with love upon me
> and deep within your eyes imparted grace,
> This mercy sets me free,
> held in your love's embrace,
> to lift my eyes adoring to your face."   (CA32)

God is always loving in the vision of Saint John of the Cross. The Living Flame of Love shows God in an eternal giving, Father to Son, Son to Father, rapt in the Spirit and guaranteeing us an infinite space or sea of love in which we can live and breathe:

> "The Father spoke one word, who was his Son,
> and this word he is always speaking in eternal silence.
> It is in silence that the soul must hear it."
>
>   (Sayings of Light and Love, 99)

Yet loneliness and a feeling of unworthiness blinds us to this vision of love. It is John's saying that if we can enter into silence, we can allow God speak his word of love to us, the love revealed in Jesus. The hard part for most is to face this silence and allow what is in us to become visible. This is the most frightening part for most. Also the writings of the New Testament are themselves works of beauty and art. Jesus did not write or leave any writings. By placing ourselves before the text we see that it can become alive today. The beauty of love revealed in the sacred writings can enrapture us in love. The lives and words of people like St. John of the Cross teach us that Jesus lives today and is ever at work. God's creative act is a present event. The event is as gentle, and as loving, as the gaze of the one who cares. When the Father gazes on us he sees us in his Son.

Paul says "You are God's temple" (2 Cor 6:16). This God lives in us and our journey is to be with this one who loves us:

> "Be glad, find joy there, gathered together and present to him
> who dwells within, since he is so close to you; desire him
> there, adore him there, and do not go off looking for him
> elsewhere...There is just one thing: even though he is within
> you, he is hidden."   (CB1:7f)

The journey of this work is to accept our loneliness, but by looking at Jesus (Heb 12:2) we can allow God transform us and heal us.

Life of St. John of the Cross (1542-1591)

He was born Juan de Yepes y Álvarez into a Converso family in Fontiveros, near Avila. Spain at the time had discovered the New World and its riches. In Spain the Jewish population had been expelled except for those who converted. John was born into a family that had converted. At the same time the 'Moors' had been defeated and with the arm of the Spanish Inquisition there was one Spain with one faith. His father Gonzalo died when John was young. Catalina, his mother, had never been accepted by Gonzalo's family. She kept her own family together in spite of poverty and hunger, finally finding work as a weaver in Medina del Campo in 1551. There was a school called 'Colejio de la Doctrina' where poor children were educated. Later under the eye of the parish priest he helped at the local hospital. He entertained the patients by telling them stories and singing songs. He loved to make people laugh, and to lift their spirits with music. John was a person of great tenderness and sensitivity, sharing the suffering of others. He saw all his patients as real people. Don Alvarez, the parish priest, offered to let Juan pursue his education at a newly founded Jesuit school, John was thrilled. In 1563 after he finished his studies he decided to join the Carmelites.

John's lot wasn't much different from the patients he looked after. All the tragedies, deaths and sufferings of his family must have made him think. It would only be at the end of his life that all these strands would come together.

John went on to Salamanca after his novitiate. There he studied theology and philosophy. John was ordained a priest in 1567 and then indicated his intent to join the Carthusian order. However, in Medina del Campo he met Teresa of Jesus (later St. Teresa of Avila) and she spoke to him about her reformation programs for the order. Teresa asked John to delay his entry and to follow her. John set out to work in Duruelo ad Pastrana. Around this time, while praying in the monastery of the Incarnation in Avila, John had a vision of the crucified Christ which led him to create his famous drawing of Christ "from above".

The years 1575-77 were years of tension between the different groups of Carmelites. John was kidnapped by some Carmelite friars. John was taken to the Carmelite monastery in Toledo. He was kept in jail in the monastery under a hated regime that included public lashing and severe isolation in a tiny cell measuring ten feet by six feet, barely large enough for his body. I have always found it strange how religious groups can be so hard like this. What notion of authority did they have? How had they become so divorced from the message of Jesus and the sacred writings? The questions are as pertinent today as then. Teresa wrote to many including the King but it was to no avail. John was weak due to lack of food and dysentery.

The worst of all was that during this ordeal John experienced the feeling of the loss of God. The absence was total. It seemed to John that his entire life, past and present, were wasted. He could no longer pray. He felt abandoned in his degradation. He was terribly ill. Many years later John would seem to be recalling this experience when he described the purifying flame of God and observed that

> "...a person suffers great deprivation and feels heavy afflictions in the spirit that ordinarily overflow into the senses, for this flame is extremely oppressive. In this preparatory purgation the flame is not bright for a person, but dark.... It is not gentle, but afflictive. Even though it sometimes imparts the warmth of love, it does so with torment and pain. And it is not delightful,... but it is consuming and contentious, making a person faint and suffer with self-knowledge... A person suffers from sharp trials in the intellect, severe dryness and distress in the will, and from the burdensome knowledge of their own miseries in the memory... In the substance of the soul they suffer abandonment, supreme poverty, dryness, cold.... They find relief in nothing, nor does any thought console them, so oppressed are they by this flame.... it truly seems to the soul that God has become displeased with it and cruel."   (Living Flame, 1:19-20)

John was crushed and destroyed. He experienced strange thoughts and desires. Everything seemed to be dragging him down. However John overcame this darkness and it was here he composed his most beautiful poetry. John's Toledo imprisonment gave to the symbol "night" its full weight. In his works this symbol is able to carry humanity's pain, able to hold even such a sense of alienation from God that the inner person feels dismantled – "like one who is imprisoned in a dark dungeon, bound hand and foot, unable to move or see or feel any favour from heaven or earth" (2N 7:3).

John did find a friend who helped him and he made his escape and reached Teresa's sisters. John was upset but came to himself and began to heal over time. Through his experience of the night he had come to know God at a deeper level. He said

> "Contemplation is nothing but a hidden, peaceful, loving inflow of God. If it is given room it will inflame the spirit with love."   (1A 13:11)

Initially we feel the pain of the night but light comes with the dawn. John has experienced his Easter-day. We remember the Easter-song

> "This is the night when Jesus Christ
> broke the chain of death
> and rose triumphant from the grave...
> The power of this holy night
> dispels all evil, washes guilt away."   (Exultet)

This Jesus is alive and was with John in his dark night leading him from darkness to light. The power of the Holy Spirit transformed John's suffering and brought to him a new life in God. John's creative period began after this. He wrote commentaries on his poetry. He was also involved in the administration of the new order of the reform. Towards the end of his life John found the order was going in a different way than he had hoped for and he found himself an outsider. He fell ill and died in Úbeda in 1591. The man in charge, Padre Francisco Crisostomo, was hostile to John when he came to Úbeda, but John's kindness changed him and he begged John for forgiveness at his death-bed. While the friars were praying for him when he died, he asked them instead to read to him from the 'Song of Songs', his favourite book in the Bible.

'Night' for Kierkegaard was his profound loneliness. 'Night' for Van Gogh was his mental anguish. The 'night' is another name for the vocation of the suffering servant (Is 52:13-53:12). The suffering servant begins:-

Who has believed what we
　　have heard?
And to whom had the arm of
　　the Lord been revealed?
For he grew up before him like a
　　young plant,
　and like a root out of dry
　　　ground;
he had no form or majesty that
　　we should look at him,
　nothing in his appearance the
　　we should desire him.
He was despised and rejected by
　　others;
　a man of suffering and
　　acquainted with infirmity;
and as one from whom others
　　hide their faces
　he was despised, and we held
　　him of now account.　　　(Is 53:1-4)

This is the text that Van Gogh had in his Bible opened in his "Still Life with
Open Bible" (1883).

The Night Belongs to Love:

John described the region of the night as an experience of Hell. "Sometimes
this experience [the night] is so vivid that it seems to the soul that it sees
Hell and perdition open before it. They are the ones who go down into Hell
alive". [N2:6;6]. He says again "… in truth the soul experiences the
sorrows of Hell, all of which reflect the feeling of God's absence, of being
chastised and rejected by him… The soul experiences this and even more
for it seems that this affliction will last forever." (N2:6, 2-3 cf N2:7, 4).
When John speaks of the soul, he means who a person most deeply is; the
essential spiritual nature of a human being.

We live in a world of shifting sands whereby things we were told and
believed in are suddenly completely undermined. Life can seem hopeful

and purposeful then something happens that breaks us. It can be an illness, humiliation and bullying at work, a friend who betrays us, or the failure of a relationship. It can be abuse, whether sexual, physical or psychological. These abuses have often left me with the feeling of being completely alone, the experience of Hell John described above. Life seems far from God and his concern. Yet John, because of his experience, is a guide for the lonely because he has been there.

John describes God's spirit of love as always working. He uses the image of fire on wood. He calls the Holy Spirit the 'Living Flame of Love'. This love penetrates and heals the soul. "Its effect is like that of fire on wood. First, the fire blackens and dries the wood, causes it to sweat and this envelops it with smoke, but then, when it has been purified in this way, the wood is burnt through from within and transformed into fire" (L 1:19-21; C 38; N2:10:1-4 etc.). The poem he wrote for "The Dark Night of the Soul" begins in the following way:

> So dark the night! At rest
> and hushed my house, I went with no one knowing
> upon a lover's quest
> – Ah the sheer grace! – so blest,
> my eager heart with love aflame and glowing.
>
> In darkness, hid from sight
> I went by secret ladder safe and sure
> – Ah grace of sheer delight! –
> so softly veiled by night,
> hushed now my house, in darkness and secure.

John's journey is a journey from sense to spirit, and from spirit to Holy Spirit. Each surrender entails a dying and John calls this dying 'night'. It is a journey in uncertainty (2N 6:1). The moving force in the dark night is the Holy Spirit who never fails in his care for his people (LF 3:46). John directed people to where the Spirit of God breathed freely – the words of sacred scripture and of his community, the Church. We find the Father loves all creation and especially humankind in the Son by the power of the Holy Spirit.

> Through the night God gathers together all the strength, the possibilities and longings of the soul... so that this total

harmony can commit its strength and power to this love. In this way, she will come to fulfill truly the first commandment, which says – rejecting nothing that is human and excluding nothing human from this love – You shall love the Lord your God with all your heart and with all your soul....

(2N 11:4)

In the midst of loneliness and darkness the soul can feel a certain companionship, a presence which gives her inner strength (2N 11:7).

We cannot heal ourselves at a deep level. In the Night we discover inner weakness. John speaks of those who get overly-angry at their brokenness:

"Many make resolutions and plans, but as they are not humble and have no distrust of themselves, the more resolutions they make the further they fall, and the more annoyed they become. They do not have the patience to wait till God gives them what they seek when he so desires..." (1N 5:3)

This runs against gentleness of spirit. I found consolation in John's witty comment on patience:

"Some people, however, are so patient about their desire to go forward, that God would prefer to see them a little less so."

(1N 5:3)

The battle in the end is God's and we have to surrender to his action in the Soul.

"It is fitting that the person do what she can, so that God will put her in the divine surgery, where she is healed of all of which she could not heal herself, she cannot by her own effort purify herself so as to be disposed in the least part for the divine union of perfect love, if God does not take her hand."

(1n 3:3)

God is love and when we enter the relationship of love and surrender to God in Christ then we allow the healing begin. I know that I am impatient but I also know that like a plant that grows, it takes time and we must wait.

God reveals his love in Jesus and those who met him spoke of how he was greater than all the ones they had known (see Matt 12:6-42; Mk 10:32). Jesus reveals to us in his person the Father's love and he gives us the Holy Spirit so that we can share this love.

The love of God comes quietly in the night. It is a fountain that flows by night:

> "I know so well the fountain, rushing and flowing
> though it be night.
> That everlasting fountain comes concealed
> in this living bread, to give us life
> though it be night."

The fountain is ocean-sized and full of love, the Father pours this love into his Son who returns love in his self-surrendering to the Father. The water of love, the Holy Spirit spills out on all creation. John's images help break down one of the barriers people put in the way of receiving this love. They say God cannot love me but John says that is not the nature of God, for him not to love would be for him to contradict himself. This is the love to which John bears witness – a God who loves us first, with a love that creates good in us and heals us. From our loneliness love creates new capacities in us.

John encourages us to view all the struggles and difficulties of life. He says in the Flame:

> "When you are burdened, you are joined to God. He is your strength and he is with people who suffer. When there is no burden you are just with yourself, your own weakness. It is in the difficulties, which test our patience, that the virtue and strength of the soul is increased and affirmed."
>
> (LF 2:30)

Here we have an echo of St. Paul who said: "We are well aware that God works with those who love him, those who have been called in accordance with his purpose and turns everything to their good. He decided beforehand those who were predestined to be moulded according to the image of his Son..." (Rom 8:28f) In pain and loneliness God opens a space for his coming. The Holy Spirit has the power to unlock in us by love, what we cannot do by ourselves. John compares us to little children who are growing up. John's own night involved unjust imprisonment when he was thirty-five and a campaign of libel against him when he was forty-nine. In the case of others he applies the language of the 'night' to situations such as loneliness, being let down by friends, being misjudged and ill-treated and frictions in family or communities (1N 9:3). He also allows for depression (LB 2:27). Everybody can make their own additions.

Paul says: "I consider that the sufferings of the present time are not worth comparing with the glory about to be revealed to us" (Rom 8:18). We groan as we await the release of pain and our groaning is part of the groaning of all creation as it awaits healing. In Revelation chapters 21 and 22 we have described for us the new Jerusalem where every tear will be wiped away (Rev 21:4) and he will be eternally with us. Our sufferings form part of the sufferings of all creation until God wins his final victory.

John says "the centre of the soul is God" (LF 1:12). We become truly ourselves in giving ourselves to God and entering into a community of love with him… In the dark night the soul can find it has lost God or is rejected by him (1N 14:1-3). John experienced this silence of God in his prison cell. It seemed as if he was in hell and everything seemed to him dark as chaos (2N 6:2,6). He was hell. All inside him seemed rotten. He felt the pangs of deep loneliness and worthlessness. It was here he met God.

The completed picture is only seen in God, for only in him do all the individual parts come together. John cites the Book of Wisdom:– "… The Spirit of the Lord has filled the whole world, and that which holds all things together knows what is said" (Wis 1:7). The Spirit of God "does the testimony to God, that, in themselves, all things give" rings forth in the music that homages the individual voices (CA 14: 1-4). God is love and our hearts rest in his love. John had this centre of spiritual gravity years before Newton's law of gravitation. Love transforms the beloved and makes him beautiful. We see ourselves as God envisions us. One of the disciples of John of the Cross was Thérèse of Lisieux (+1890). She experienced a dark night of loneliness, like Jesus in Hell. She felt totally alone and abandoned, yet she faced this 'night' with faith and love. For all who have come in contact with Thérèse they feel something of the 'love' she had become and she gives hope to those who feel helpless.

John speaks of the beauty of the love of God which enraptures us and calls us to be sharers in:

> "…and let us go forth to behold ourselves in your beauty. This means, that we should be like one another in beauty and that this occurs in your beauty, so that when one looks at the other, you alone appear in your beauty, and each sees the other in your beauty, which happens when you transform me into your beauty; hence I shall see you in your beauty, and you shall see me in your beauty, and I shall see myself in you in your beauty, and you shall see yourself in me in your beauty; and I will resemble you in your beauty, and you resemble me in your beauty, and my beauty shall be your beauty, and your beauty my beauty; wherefore I shall be you in your beauty, and you shall be me in your beauty, because your very beauty shall be my beauty." (CA, 35:2)

Coming to Know God:

> "The capacity of these caverns [the human spirit] is deep, because that which can fill them is deep, infinite and that is God. So in a sense their capacity will be infinite; so their thirst is infinite, and their hunger is deep and infinite, and their sense of pain and disintegration is infinite death, when the soul is about to receive what will fill it" (LF 3:22).

We must seek God in faith and love (CB 1:11) and through faith and hope we await God. Love is the way to God (see 1 Cor 13) and the "soul's health is the love of God" (CB 11:11).

Pink Floyd in the album "The Dark Side of the Moon" in the tracks 'Brain Damage, the Lunatic' said "there's someone in my head and it's not me'. Our memories can be like that. Negative voices from the past can haunt us. In coming to face the faceless voices in meditation and before God divests these voices of their power. The gentle inflow of love gives us hope and new belief in God and ourselves.

Love heals our hurting. The Holy Spirit has power to turn every wound into wounds of love (LF 2:7). Love decodes the meaning of the world which

John reads as a limitless sea of love all around him (LF 2:10). John says: When a person has no love, she is dead (Sayings 114, 2A24:5-7 etc.).

In beholding God revealed in Jesus as love we are transformed by love. "... He loves us that we might love him, through the love he has for us" (Letter 33 to a Carmelite nun). The activity of God's inflowing love is the work of the Holy Spirit. Love is the very gift of God coming into our hearts: "Hope does not disappoint us, because God's love has been poured into our hearts by the Holy Spirit who has been given to us" (Rom 5:5). John says:

> "It is by love that the soul is united with God... so for the person to be in her centre, which is God, it is sufficient for her to have one degree of love, because by just one degree the soul is united with him by grace." (LB1:13)

God's company, says John, does not rest until he makes us fit for his company. God's aim is to make us gods by participation, as he is God by nature – like fire turning everything to fire. It creates a likeness to the one who loves (see 2N 13:9; CB 12:7-8, 32:6). For God to gaze is to love and when he looks upon us ('gazes') he loves us. His look of love makes a person beautiful.

> "You looked with love upon me
> and deep within, your eyes imprinted grace;
> this mercy sets me free,
> held in your love's embrace,
> to lift my eyes adoring to your face."   (CA 32)

This explains the angle John (followed by Dalí) saw Jesus at in his depiction of the crucifixion. It is as if one is seeing the figure of Jesus as from above from the point of view of the Father. He loves us in the Son and sees us as his children in the Son. "When we cry 'Abba', Father, it is that very Spirit bearing witness with our spirit that we are children of God" (Rom 8:15f). This is John's vision – a God constantly gazing in love upon the universe, personally meeting us if we allow him. Love is a supreme value and can save the world:

> "A little of this pure love is more precious to God, more precious for the soul, and of more benefit to the church, even

though it seems to be doing nothing, than all those other good works put together... it is for this goal of love that we were created." (CB 29: 2-3; LF 1:3)

John explains his attitude towards Jesus in the Ascent and this helps us understand that to understand John we have to look at Jesus and him crucified. The event of Jesus being born in time and space leads to the cross where Jesus says "It is accomplished" (Jn 19:20). He has overcome sin and alienation with love. This has been the idea of God through the Old Testament as far as Jesus (2A 22:7). The beauty of love that Jesus reveals will come to life in us. "All are mine and all mine yours; and I have been glorified in them" (Jn 17:10). We are God's adopted children in Jesus (CA 35:5). John puts the following words into the mouth of the Father:

"If you desire to answer with a word of comfort, behold my Son subject to me and to others out of love for me and you will see how much He answers you. If you desire me to declare some secret truths or events to you, fix your eyes on Him and you will discern in Him the most secret mysteries, and wisdom, and the wonders of God..." (2A 22:6)

He goes on to quote the Letter to the Colossians where Paul says "In the Son of God are hidden all the treasures and the wisdom of God" (Col 2:3). Paul after his transformation says he knew no other than Jesus Christ and him crucified (1 Cor 2:2). This is where we come to know God revealed in Jesus when we behold him who was crucified because "in Christ all the fullness of the divinity dwells" (Col 2:9). (2A 22:6). Jesus has passed from death to life in God and he is with us to lead us to life. It is by beholding his sacrifice of love that we can enter this mystery. We are drawn into this love by the Holy Spirit and we enter the heart of God and become his children and partners in healing the world. He was influenced by the writings of St. Bonaventure (+1274) and the figure of St. Francis (+1226) in coming to see God as a living fire of love. This is the love that heals us.

John's aim in facing the night is to follow Jesus. St. Paul says: "Not that I have achieved this or already achieved the goal but I press on to make it my own, because Jesus Christ has made me his own..." (Phil 3:12ff). Paul regards everything else as loss compared to the supreme knowledge of Jesus Christ (Phil 3:7). "I want to know Christ and the power of his resurrection and the sharing of his sufferings by becoming like him in death, if somehow I may attain the resurrection of the dead" (Phil 3:10f). John uses the words 'Christ', 'Word', 'Son', 'Lord' to refer to Jesus the Christ. He also refers to him as the bridegroom.

In the letter to the Romans Paul writes: "There is therefore no condemnation for those who are in Christ Jesus" (Rom 8:1). For him "in Christ" means a deep communion, heart to heart, with Jesus. As we move more and more towards this union our lives are permeated with love. Paul speaks with great confidence of this love:

> What then are we to say about these things? If God is for us, who is against us? He who did not withhold his own Son, but gave him up for all of us, will he not with him also give us everything else? Who will bring any charge against God's elect? It is God who justifies. Who is to condemn? It is Christ Jesus, who died, yes, who was raised, who is at the right hand of God, who indeed intercedes for us. Who will separate us from the love of Christ? Will hardship, or distress, or persecution, or famine, or nakedness, or peril, or sword? As it is written,
>> "For your sake we are being
>> killed all day long;
>> we are accounted as sheep to
>> be slaughtered."
>
> No, in all these things we are more than conquerors through him who loved us. For I am convinced that neither death, nor life, nor angels, nor rulers, nor things present, nor things to come, nor powers, nor height, nor depth, nor anything else in all creation, will be able to separate us from the love of God in Christ Jesus our Lord.   (Rom 8:31-39)

God's love has been shown in Jesus the Christ. On the cross and in the resurrection it is an experienced fact. Paul is stating 'God is for us' – he goes on to argue that nothing can take away the love God has for us and the love he revealed in Jesus. God has forgiven us and reconciled us in Christ and poured out his love into our hearts through the Holy Spirit (Rom 5:5). In praying and contemplating passages like this we are led into the very heart of God.

For John, Jesus and union with him is the place from which we can come to love the Father without measure. We love him anew and with great delight through his son Jesus Christ. And this she does united with Christ, together with Christ (CB 37:6). Yet he is aware that Christ was 'annihilated', 'deserted' and 'crucified' and it is with Christ who is now alive that we face the 'night' and await the new life of the Spirit.

It was in silence and prayer where John received his focus and strength.

> "In all our needs, struggles and difficulties, we shall find no better, no surer way of going forward than prayer and the hope that God will provide in the way he desires. When means fail us and we see no way of dealing with our difficulties, it only remains for us to lift our eyes to You, so that You may provide as You see best."   (2A 21:5)

Our basic attitude is 'ask' and 'trust'. St. Paul reminds us: "Likewise the Spirit helps us in our weakness, for we do not know how to pray as we ought, but that Spirit intercedes with sighs too deep for words. And God, who searches the heart, knows what is in the mind of the Spirit, because the Spirit intercedes for the saints according to the mind of God" (Rom 8:26f). We are in the Spirit when we pray and he helps us when we cannot find words. The Spirit is the love that transforms us. He is God's empowering presence. John knows this and he asks us to 'trust' because God is ever faithful. He will hear our prayer. The crucified love of Jesus opens the world to the gift of the Holy Spirit; that love which is at work in prayer. John tells us to pray in the living temple of the soul (CB 17:10). In the Gospel of John we hear Jesus say: "Anyone who loves me will keep my word and my Father will love him and we shall come to him and make our home in him" (Jn 14:23). God dwells in our hearts and our prayer is a being-with this God who is closer to us than we are to ourselves. We meet in a spiritual way, heart to heart, when we pray in faith and love. John says

> "Be glad, find joy there, gathered together and present to him who dwells within, since he is so close to you; desire him there, adore him there and do not go off looking elsewhere."
>   (CB 1:7-8)

It is by the work of the Holy Spirit that this loving union is found. God's indwelling is the work of the Holy Spirit. As we grow in love we become more and more moved by the Holy Spirit. For St. Paul being 'in Christ' is the same as the term 'in the Spirit'. We grow in love by the indwelling of the Holy Spirit:

> "it can only attain this likeness [to Jesus] by a total transformation of its will into the will of God... This does not destroy the soul's will; it becomes God's will. Thus it loves God with the will of God, which is its own will: now it loves as much as it is loved, for it loves with the divine will, that is, through the Holy Spirit." (CA 37)

So the breathing of the Holy Spirit by the Father and the Son becomes the breathing of the soul. We see he is love, a love that is eternal. We become truly ourselves and enter a new life in the Spirit.

> The Spirit forms and equips the soul so that, in God, it can carry out the same breathing of love that the Father fulfills in the Son and the Son in the Father. This breathing of love is the same Holy Spirit whom they breathe forth to one another in this transformation. For the transformation would not be genuine if the soul were not unveiledly and patently refashioned into the three Persons of the Most Holy Trinity... The soul breathes God in God, and this breathing is the breathing of God himself... It must not be thought impossible for the soul to desire something so sublime, for if God gives it grace to become God-like and united to the Most Holy Trinity, and so become God by participation, why should we not believe that it attains its insight, its knowledge and its love within the Trinity and in participation in the Trinity, just as the latter does itself... [albeit through] participation, since God is at work in it? (CA 39: 3-6)

Chapter 7

God's Lonely Man

In the deeply disturbing film 'Apocalypse Now' we hear Kurtz (played by Marlon Brando) read T.S. Eliot's 'The Hollow Man'. He knows Willard is coming to kill him and he awaits his fate ready. When he reads he leaves out the line "Mistah Kurtz, he dead". Kurtz in the film is facing his death. He is already dead morally and is "hollow". The film is based on Joseph Conrad's 'Heart of Darkness' (1899). The heart of darkness is a metaphor for evil. The heart has no compassion, no empathy. It thrives on cruelty and domination. Kurtz possesses this heart. So too, does Willard. In the film he identifies with Kurtz. In one scene he shoots an innocent woman. He doesn't flinch or show emotion. The rest of his crew are part of the dehumanising war, but they react with shock. Willard doesn't, he is in the grip of the Heart of Darkness. He kills Kurtz and the people who worshipped Kurtz now turn their allegiance to Willard. The Heart of Darkness lives on in him and the power of evil attracts like people. T.S. Eliot wrote 'The Hollow Man' in the 1920's. His is a post-war experience. At the same time his marriage had failed and his wife descended into mental illness.

The poem begins:

> Mistah Kurtz - he dead
>   A penny for the Old Guy
>
> We are the hollow men
> We are the stuffed men
> Leaning together
> Headpiece filled with straw. Alas!
> Our dried voices, when
> We whisper together
> Are quiet and meaningless
> As wind in dry grass

Or rats' feet over broken glass
In our dry cellar

Shape without form, shade without colour,
Paralysed force, gesture without motion;

Those who have crossed
With direct eyes, to death's other Kingdom
Remember us - if at all - not as lost
Violent souls, but only
As the hollow men
The stuffed men.

We already saw that "Mistah Kurtz, he dead" refers to Joseph Conrad's 'Heart of Darkness'. The guy is the straw effigy that is burned on Guy Fawkes night in England.

The poem begins properly "We are the hollow men". The hollow ones aren't people over there that we can look down on. No! says Eliot, we are the hollow ones. There is nothing inside except useless straw. Our lives are filled with trivia. We are addicted to social media (after Eliot's time, of course) but we say nothing. Eliot wrote in 1925, yet his words hold true for the 21st century. We are hollow as if we were encased in our own indifference. There is no empathy, no compassion, no love. There is no humanity. When we look around we see empty faces, forced smiles. People are lonely are are vainly trying to convince themselves that they are not. We are the hollow men!

Later in the poem Eliot refers to Dante's Inferno. In Canto III of the Inferno, Dante speaks of the vestibule of hell. This is peopled by sad people who are not great sinners. They are too indifferent. Nor are they saints, because they don't really care. One group of hollow ones are the group who follow aimlessly a man who carries a meaningless flag. These are the people who follow empty slogans in society. These slogans can be political, social, religious – Hitler once said: "It is as well for politicians that the people do not think." The mindless following of slogans, fashion or whatever is the in-thing typifies so many of the hollow ones. We are the hollow ones! Indifference reigns and because of this cruelty abounds. The poem finishes with some of the most quoted lines in literature:

> For Thine is
>> Life is
>> For Thine is the
>
>> This is the way the world ends
>> This is the way the world ends
>> This is the way the world ends
>> Not with a bang but a whimper.

The hollow men try to remember a half-forgotten prayer. They speak some lines from the Our Father, but can get nowhere. They see the world end 'not with a bang, but with a whimper'. Cold indifference and hollowness allow the world and its children die. Countless numbers of innocent die every day because we remain silent. We are hollow!

Taxi Driver is a 1976 film directed by Martin Scorsese with Paul Schrader doing the screenplay. The hero or more appropriately anti-hero is Travis Bickle, played by Robert De Niro. Travis is the epitome of loneliness. Thomas Wolfe (+1938) wrote "the whole conviction of my life now rests upon the belief that loneliness, far from being a rare and curious phenomenon, is the central and inevitable font of human existence (God's Lonely Man). Travis feels this loneliness acutely. "Loneliness followed me my whole life everywhere", he says. "In bars, in cars, sidewalks, stores, everywhere. I am God's lonely man". He lives inside his head, a dark, paranoid and lonely place. His loneliness and alienation is often communicated by the camera-angles used by Scorsese. The shots are a commentary on a lonely, paranoid mind. Travis is afflicted by self-loathing. This leads him to self-destructive patterns in his life. He tries to bond with 'Betsy', played by Cybill Shepherd, but he sabotages the relationship, making sure the relationship fails. This reinforces Travis's loneliness and self-loathing. Travis hates the world and the people he finds. Yet in his taxi he works nights and spends his time seeking out the violence of the night. He reinforces his negative view of humanity in this way. He looks for a meaning, something to give him purpose. His paranoia leads him to attempt to become a killer. He changes his haircut to a mohawk haircut. This was the haircut used by special troops in Vietnam who were on a special mission in the jungle. He attempts to kill Senator Palantine (Leonard Harris) but he fails. Instead he kills Sport (Harvey Keitel) who uses Iris (Jodie Foster) as a child prostitute. Travis becomes a hero, but it was only by chance that he killed Sport and his gang. Originally he had intended to kill Senator Palantine. In the end we are left wondering where and what will Travis do next. We are not told. The film ends.

The Hollow men, Kurtz, Willard, and Travis Bickle serve as mirrors and warnings to us. Once Paul Schrader was talking to a man who suddenly said to him, "How did you know me? Why did you make a film about me?" Schrader was taken aback and asked the man did he drive a taxi, the man replied no, but insisted the film was about him. In a way he was right. Travis is a lonely man, locked inside of himself. Yet he cooperates in his own loneliness. He shows us the confused shadow part of ourselves. it is as if Scorsese is saying to us through Travis, we don't have to surrender to the darkness. The Heart of Darkness and Apocalypse Now serve as warnings, not just as moments for reflection. They show us the dark parts of ourselves. They enable us accept this part and seek ways to abort our loneliness. Conrad, Coppola and Scorsese did it through their art. We are God's work of art and when we can accept the dark side of ourselves then we can grow in God. As Leonard Cohen said:

> "There is a crack in everything
> That's how the light gets in"
>
> (Anthem, 1992)

The poet Rumi says:

> "The wound is the place where the light enters you."

The Light of the World:

Jesus says "I am the light of the world (John 8:12). As we meditate on the Cross of Dali and John of the Cross we allow his love enter us. St. Paul tells us "... anyone who attaches himself to the Lord is one spirit with him" (1 Cor 6:17). We come to share in his Spirit and allow his love enter where there was darkness. Jesus involves us in his mission of love. This is our dignity in our new life in Christ. That is why St. Paul says there is no condemnation for those in Christ Jesus (Romans 8:1).

Karl Barth in his Church Dogmatics examined what the faith said about Jesus. There is a story told of Barth (apocryphal, no doubt). One day a student fell asleep in his class. When he awoke Barth asked him could he sum up what the lecture had been about. The student thought and said "Jesus Christ". "Correct" said a delighted Barth.

In his Church Dogmatics, his lifetime's work, he saw God at work in Jesus Christ through his humanity in the power of the Holy Spirit. Jesus is the Emmanuel, God with us. Participation in Christ is a history in which creatures transcend their limits by becoming genuinely human. Barth says: "God has something specific to say to each man, something that applies to him and him alone" (CD III/2:159). God is always gracious. He reconciles us to himself and involves us in Christ in his saving work. This is our dignity.

> "In faith man is in conformity to God, i.e. capable of receiving God's word, capable of so corresponding in his own decision to the decision God has made about him in the Word that the Word is now the Word heard by him and he himself is now the man addressed by this Word."
>
> (CD III/2:179)

Finding ourselves in an I-Thou relationship releases us from loneliness. By our wounds we can let the light in. We can hear the words of love addressed to us by God in Jesus. We become truly human. God's love is the Holy Spirit and tells us our part. As Barth says:

For the gift and work of the Holy Spirit as the divine power of His Word is that, while Jesus Christ encounters man in it with alien majesty, He does not remain thus, nor is He merely a strange, superior Lord disposing concerning him in majesty from without. On the contrary, even as such, without ceasing to be the Lord or forfeiting His transcendence, but rather in its exercise, He gives and imparts Himself to him, entering into him as his Lord in all His majesty and setting up His throne within him. Thus His control, as that of the owner over his possession, becomes the most truly distinctive feature of this man, the centre and basis of his human existence, the axiom of his freest thinking and utterance, the origin of his freest volition and action, in short the principle of his spontaneous being [Prinzip seines spontanen Daseins]. The gift and work of the Holy Spirit as the divine power of the Word of vocation is the placing of man in this fellowship with Him, namely, with the being, will and action of Jesus Christ.

(CD IV/3:2:538)

Thus as Jesus Christ encounters those whom he calls, he illuminates and awakens them to their true being – a being in the freedom of his service. In so doing he becomes the ruling principle of their lives, and as such he awakens them to the freedom and spontaneity of their own truest selves.

(ibid).

We find our true humanity in Christ and our vocation in him. Sin for Barth is when we refuse to become human and instead become nothing. Von Balthasar (+1988) used some of the same ideas in his Theodrama. To be a person for Von Balthasar means fulfilling the role or mission God has called the individual to perform. It is in union with Christ and by the power of the Holy Spirit that we discover the mission we are called to. In fulfilling this mission we become the persons God has called us to be. We see this in the case of St. Thérèse of Lisieux. By surrendering herself into the hands of God and seeking to fulfill his will, she truly became the person she was called to be.

Jesus dying on the cross and his resurrection ushered in a new age. He has started a new creation (2 Cor 5:17) and this ultimately results in the new heaven and the new earth (Rev 21:1). Jesus Christ, the new Adam, opens up an area of Christian mission, in which the Christian, en Christo (in Christ), can be seen to have a share in the salvific work and suffering for the world. The completeness of "what is lacking in Christ's afflictions for the sake of the body, that is, the Church" (Col 1:24) takes place in faith, but it can also be experienced by those with certain mystical gifts (TD3, p. 241): God has left a unique role for each of us to perform. That is our great dignity. In the Book of Revelation this dignity is symbolised by the stone and the manna:

> "Let anyone who can hear, listen to what the Spirit is saying to the churches: to those who prove victorious I will give some hidden manna and a white stone, with a new name written on it, known only to the person who receives it."
>
> (Rev 2:17)

St. Francis shows this development. As a young man he had sought fame and glory, but he was disappointed in his enterprises and found himself ill, lonely and depressed. This was the crack where he let the light come in. He withdrew to lonely places and caves where he spent hours in prayer. He brought a friend with him so as to keep his sanity. In this way he reached out for help. Think of Travis Bickle, this is what he did not do. In prayer Francis was transformed (see 1 Cel 7). In the church of San Damiano St. Francis came to know the love of God revealed in Jesus as he meditated on the Crucifix there. He became one with Christ in his lifetime. The love of God was poured into his heart by the Holy Spirit (Rom 5:5). He came to bear the wounds of Christ on his body towards the end of his life. He had a universal compassion and love for all. That is why so many were drawn to him. Earlier we saw how people were drawn to the Heart of Darkness. The heart of love, too, reaches out and gives life. The heart of darkness brings death. St. John of the Cross spoke of the transforming fire of the Holy Spirit's love. He wrote of St. Francis and his transformation in love:

Let us return to the work of that seraph, for he truly inflicts a sore, and wounds inwardly in the spirit. Thus, if God sometimes permits an effect to extend to the bodily senses in the fashion in which it existed interiorly, the wound and sore appear outwardly, as happened when the seraph wounded St. Francis. When his soul was wounded with love by the five wounds, their effect extended to the body, and these wounds were impressed on the body, which was wounded just as his soul was wounded with love.

God usually does not bestow a favour on the body without bestowing it first and principally on the soul. Thus the greater the delight and strength of love the wound produces in the soul, so much greater is that produced by the wound outside on the body, and when there is an increase in one there is an increase in the other. This so happens because these souls are purified and established in God, and what is a cause of pain and torment to their corruptible flesh is sweet and delectable to their strong and healthy spirit. It is, then, a wonderful thing, experiencing the pain augmented with the delectable.

(LF 2:13)

The love of God poured into the heart by the Holy Spirit (Rom 5:5) enables one to see the world and its people with God's eyes. The cross of Dalí we have meditated on shows us Jesus looking on the world with love and compassion. His are the eyes of God looking on us his people. When we share his love by the power of the Holy Spirit, John tells us:

The soul feels its ardour strengthen and increase and its love become so refined in this ardour that seemingly there flow seas of loving fire within it, reaching to the heights and depths of the earthly and heavenly spheres, imbuing all with love. It seems to it that the entire universe is a sea of love in which it is engulfed, for conscious of the living point or centre of love within itself, it is unable to catch sight of the boundaries of this love.

There is nothing else to say about the soul's enjoyment here except that it realises how appropriately the kingdom of heaven was compared in the Gospel to a grain of mustard seed that, by reason of its intense heat, grows into a large tree, despite its being so small (Mt. 13:31-32). For the soul beholds itself converted into the immense fire of love that emanates from that enkindled point at the heart of the spirit.

(LF 2:10)

St. Francis experienced this love and he led others to find it in their lives. In his healing many were healed. We are called to share in this love. For some it might seem like a winter season of the Spirit. Yet it is here we meet God in Jesus. We can hear his voice and share in his spirit of love. John of the Cross speaks of the passing of this winter and the new life of Spring, quoting the Song of Songs. He says:

Moreover, a soul is conscious that in the vigour of the Bridegroom's delightful communication the Holy Spirit rouses and invites it by the immense glory he marvelously and with gentle affection places before its eyes, telling it what he told the bride in the Song of Songs. The bride thus refers to this: Behold what my Spouse is saying to me: *Arise and make haste, my love, my dove, my beautiful one, and come; for winter is now passed, and the rains are over and gone, and the flowers have appeared in our land; the fig tree has put forth her fruits; the vines in flower have given their fragrance. Arise, my love, my fair one, and come; my dove in the clefts of the rock, in the hollow of the wall, show me your face, let your voice sound in my ears, because your voice is sweet and your face beautiful* [Sg. 2:10-14].

(LF 1:28)

We too, if we live with our loneliness for a time, will hear the voice telling us that winter is past.

Just One Look:

St. John of the Cross' depiction of the cross (followed by Dalí) has been with us throughout. The angle of the figure on the cross is expressive. We see Jesus from above, from the Father's angle. Jesus looks in love and embraces all of humanity. He wants all people to be saved (1 Tim 2:4). God sees us through the eyes of Jesus and loves us through Jesus and in Jesus. When we perceive this look of love we enter a world where we are healed. We are also called to bear that love to others. St. Paul tells us "… anyone who attaches himself to the Lord is one spirit with him" (1 Cor:17).

"In Jesus":

In the letter to the Ephesians we read

> "Blessed be God,
> The Father of our Lord Jesus Christ,
> who has blessed us
> with all the spiritual blessings of heaven in Christ.
> Thus he chose us in Christ,
> before the world was made
> to be holy and blameless
> before him in love"

(Eph 1:1f)

'In Christ' refers to our becoming one with Christ. He unites us to himself in love according to God's election to heal us, save us and make of us a holy and living people. This is achieved by the work of the Holy Spirit, "the pledge of our inheritance" (Eph 1:14). Jesus has risen from the dead. This shows God's choice and by entering into communion with him we share in his work of healing for the world. We are enabled to do this by the breath of the Holy Spirit. This is what Paul means when he speaks of being "in Christ" (*en Christo*). "Thus condemnation will never come to those in Christ Jesus" (Rom 8:1).

This idea of union with Jesus by the power of the Spirit and our vocation within this played a large part in Karl Barth's Church Dogmatics. Barth gave great importance to God's revelation of himself in Jesus and his work of reconciling all things and people to himself by the life, death and resurrection of Jesus.

> The concrete form of this teleological power of grace is the person of Jesus Christ Himself. [A]s He is obedient to this will of God, Jesus also shows what it is that God rightly wills of us. The basic divine decision concerning man is embodied in Jesus. The determination in which man is directed to his promised future, is given in Him. Jesus Himself is the impulsion of all men to eternal life. He Himself is the claim which God has made and continually makes upon men.   (CD, II/2, p. 567)

God has chosen us "in Jesus" and as he leads Jesus to new life so he calls us to this new life. God has chosen us in Christ and his will is that we all be saved. In this way Barth overcame the idea of double predestination that was prevalent since the time of Calvin. God loves all and wills the healing and salvation of all people, even those that do not know him. Jesus gives us the Holy Spirit so we can be one with him and work with him:

> As Jesus Christ calls us and is heard by us He gives us His Holy Spirit in order that His own relationship to His Father [i.e., the relationship of obedience] may be repeated [*wiederhole*] in us [i.e., in our obedience]. He then knows us, and we know Him, as the Father knows Him and He the Father. Those who live in this repetition [*Wiederholung*] live in the Holy Spirit. The gift and work of the Holy Spirit in us is that Jesus Christ should live in us by faith, that He should be in solidarity and unity with us and we with Him, and therefore that our obedience should be necessary and our disobedience excluded.   (CD II/2, p. 780)

When we allow God's love enter our lives then Jesus lives in us. In the Gospel of John we read: "Anyone who loves me will keep my word, and my Father will love him and we shall come to him and make our home in him" (Jn 14:13). This is achieved by living in the Spirit that Jesus has given us. Living in this Spirit means we are in union with Jesus and the Father. Jesus' fulfillment of the covenant of grace establishes the context within which we as human beings are called to exist. The essence of human life is to be drawn into this special relationship Jesus has with the Father in the Spirit. Jesus, for Barth, is both transcendent lord and obedient servant.

Barth goes on to say:

> Among all other men and all other creatures He is the penetrating spearhead of the will of God their Creator: penetrating because in Him the will of God is already fulfilled and revealed, and the purpose of God for all men and creatures has thus reached its goal; and the spearhead to the extent that there has still to be a wider fulfillment of the will of God and its final consummation, and obviously this can only follow on what has already been achieved in this man. (CD, III/2, p. 143)

What God has achieved in the resurrection of Jesus is what he hopes to achieve for all humankind and all of creation, all of the universe. Jesus has overcome death by the power of God and will die no more. He now lives in loving union with the Father in the Spirit. We are called "in Jesus" to that place. St. Paul says: "We are well aware that the whole creation, to this time, has been groaning in labour pains" (Rom 8:22). We are not fully saved in time. God is working still to achieve in us and creation what he achieved in Jesus by the resurrection. Jesus came in time and space to inaugurate God's kingdom. Jesus' true humanity for Barth exists in this act of union with God. Our humanity comes to be when we enter this life of union. When we hear God's command and we seek to be in union with Jesus to fulfill it then we become human. We often contradict our own humanity but this does not dissolve the fact that Jesus Christ has claimed and secured the humanity of each of us.

This form of existing is to be found in the participation of humanity in Jesus Christ. This is what underlines our humanity. We are elected in Christ (Eph 1:1-4). This election proceeds from the humanity of Jesus Christ and is ever present in its teleological power. (CD, III/2, p. 164). It is looking into God revealed in Jesus as love that we come to know ourselves in God.

> That he is, and is therefore obedient, means that the statement: "I am," must be interpreted by the further statement: "I will." ... Man is, of course, purely receptive [*rein rezeptiv*] as regards the movement from God. ... God is Subject, but over against God and in relation to Him man is also subject. ... By willing, I recognise the fact that my being is not simply a gift with which I am endowed but a task for which I am commissioned. Indeed, I affirm and grasp my being as my task, and treat it as such.
>
> (CD, III/2, p. 179)

Each of us has a dignity and a part to play in God's healing of the world and universe. We do not often think we are called. In Barth's terms we are not really ourselves. How to explain this mystery of our value is difficult because many of us have heard voices telling us we are worthless and have suffered experiences that made us feel worthless.

Barth often spoke of what he called "secular parables". These are truths we come across in life in the world that on the one hand seem to be remote from God but at the same time contain a truth that points to the truth of the Word made flesh, Jesus Christ (see CD IV, 3.1, p. 114). This was the method used by Jesus in his parables. One such parable for me was the fate of Richard Wright (+2006) of the band Pink Floyd. During one of the fights among the band the question was asked what did Richard do for the band and in Floyd style somebody said 'nothing' and Richard was dismissed from the band he helped form. Things did not go well and bit by bit Richard was re-instated. It was only when he was gone that the others came to realise that his gentle presence and silence was something they needed. He was vital like blood in the system, even though they could not say exactly why. The business model of humanity doesn't always work. Taking this into the divine sphere God works in different ways in different people, in us if we let him. Nobody should be despised because he or she does not appear to be a powerful, charismatic figure. Barth tells us that the being of man is being in responsibility before God. We should have the character of 'obedience' to God (CD III/2, p. 179). The word obedience refers in its root to hearing what God has said and our response to this word.

In Alexandr Solzhenitsyn's (+2008) novella "Matryona's Home" he tells the story of Matryona and her sad and, in the eyes of the world, her insignificant life. Yet after she dies Solzhenitsyn wrote the following words about her:

> "We all lived beside her, and never understood that she was
> the righteous one without whom, according to the proverb,
> no village can stand.
> Nor any city.
> Nor our whole world."

In God's dispensation Matryona supported others quietly like a Mary of Nazareth. People used and abused her yet she was the one who kept decency and hope alive. She was the suffering servant of Isaiah (Is 52:13-53:12). Only in God do we truly know ourselves and others. In the Book of Revelation we read "to those who prove victorious I will give some hidden manna and a white stone with a new name written on it, known only to the person who receives it" (Rev 2:17). The new stone symbolises who we are in God's eyes.

True this vision of our humanity is different from us. In the end using the painting of John of the Cross (and Dalí) we can look at the figure of Jesus who looks on us with love. It is love that heals and calls us into the peace of our union with the Father. Here we have to linger often and allow love to enter. This is our healing. This is the cure for our loneliness, not our view of ourselves but God's view of us and his profound love for each one of us.

God is not like us. He is totally other. Barth went to great lengths to emphasise this. Our loving is imperfect but God's nature is love and light. There is a longing within each of us to experience this love. This longing is placed in our hearts by God and he uses this longing in us to lead us to him. Too often human agency leads us away from this longing and we are "not ourselves". Yet God seeks us and our profound loneliness arises from the fact that we are divided. Yet God continues to love and seek us. Our part is to remain silent and let him enter. As John says:

> "O Lord, my God, who will seek you with simple and pure love and not find that you are all one can desire, for you show yourself first and go out to meet those who seek you."
> (Sayings of Light and Love, no. 2)

Bibliography

Auden, W.H., *The Age of Anxiety* (New York: 1948)

Barth, Karl, *Anselm: Fides Quarens Intellectum* (London: 1960)

Barth, Karl, *Church Dogmatics* (Edinburgh: 1956-1975)

Barth, Karl, *The Epistle to the Romans* (In German: Der Romerbrief) (London: 1933)

Barth, Karl, *The Word of God and The Word of Man* (Gloucester, Mass: 1978)

Blumenthal, David, *Facing the Abusing God: A Theology of Protest* (Louisville: 1993)

Bernanos, George, *Diary of A Country Priest*, London, Boriswood, 1937

Brasnett, B., *The Suffering of the Impassible God* (London 1928)

Brueggemann, Walter, *The Message of the Psalms* (Minneapolis: 1984)
'From Hurt to Joy, From Death to Life' in *The Psalms and the Life of Faith* (Minneapolis: 1995)
'The Formfulness of Grief in *The Psalms and the Life of Faith* (Minneapolis: 1995)
Isaiah 40-66 (Louisville: 1998)
A Shape for Old Testament Theology I -Structure Legitimation - *Catholic Biblical Quarterly* -47 (1985) 28-46
A Shape for Old Testament Theology II - Embrace of Pain- *Catholic Biblical Quarterly* -47 (1985) 395-415
'Hopeful Imagination' (Philadelphia: 1986)

Chiolerio, M., *Lo Spirito Santo nella Preghiera*, in Enciclopedia della Preghiera (Rome: 2007)

Clapton, Eric, *Clapton: The Autobiography* (New York: 2008)

Coote, R., *Yahweh recalls Elijah,* in Traditions and Transformation (Winona Lake: 1981)

Dahood, M, *Psalms* (3 vols: Anchor Bible 16, 17,17a) (Gordon City, New York: 1966, 1968, 1970)

Davidson, Robert, *The Vitality of Worship: A Commentary on the Book of Psalms* (Edinburgh: 1998)
The Courage to Doubt (London: 1983)

Descharnes, Robert, *Dalí* (New York: 2003)

Galot, J., *Dieu souffre-t-il?* (Paris: 1976)

Heschel, Abraham J, *Man's Quest for God*
(New York: 1954)
God in Search of Man: A Philosophy of Judaism
(New York: 1955)
'On Prayer: *Conservative Judaism, 25, No 1* (Fall, 1970) 1-14
The Prophets (New York: 1962)
Who is Man? (Stanford University Press, 1965)
The Insecurity of Freedom: Essays on Human Existence
(New York: 1966)
'No Religion is an Island' in *No Religion is an Island*
(Eds. Harold Kasimow and Byron L Sherwin, Maryknoll: 1991)
A Passion for Truth (Woodstock: 1995)

Jacquet, Louis, *Les Psaumes et le Coeur de l'Homme*, 3 Vols (Brussels: 1975-1979)

Julian of Norwich, *Revelation of Divine Love*, chapter 31.

Kavanagh, Kieran & Otilio Rodriguez, *The Complete Works of St. John of the Cross* (ICS: 1991)

Kierkegaard, Soren, *The Concept of Anxiety* (New York: 2014)

Kuschel, Karl-Josef, *Born Before All Time? The Dispute over Christ's Origin* (London: 1992)

Laing, Olivia, *The Lonely City: Adventures in the Art of Being Alone* (Edinburgh: 2006)

Long, Stephen, *Saving Karl Barth: Von Balthasar's Preoccupation* (Minneapolis: 2014)

McGrath, Alister, *Christian Theology* (London, 2011)

Martelet, G., *L'au-delà Retrouvé, Christologie des fins dernières* (Paris: 1974) p. 181-188.

Mays, James L, *The Lord Reigns: A Theological Handbook to the Psalms* (Louisville John Knox Press, 1994)
Psalms: Interpretation (Louisville: 1994)

McCann, J Clinton, *A Theological Introduction to the Book of Psalms: The Psalms as Torah* (Nashville: 1993)

Miller, P D, *Interpreting the Psalms* (Philadelphia, Fortress Press, 1986)
They Cried to the Lord: The Form and Theology of Biblical Prayer (Minneapolis: 1994)

Moltmann, Jürgen, *A Broad Place* (London: 2007)

Moltmann, Jürgen, *Theology of Hope* (London: 1961)

Moltmann, Jürgen, *The Crucified God* (London: 1973)

Moltmann, Jürgen, *Why am I a Christian?* in Experiences of God (London: 1980), 1-18

Moltmann, Jürgen, *The Trinity and the Kingdom: The Doctrine of God* (London: 1980)

Moltmann, Jürgen, *The Spirit of Life: A Universal Affirmation* (London: 2009)

Naifeh, Stephen and Gregory White Smith, *Van Gogh: The Life* (New York: 2011)

Nardoni, E., *The Concept of Charism in Paul*, CBQ (55), 1993

Pannenberg, Wolfhart, *Did Jesus Really Rise from the Dead*, Dialog 4 (1965), p. 125-135

Péguy, Charles, *La Porche du Mystère de la deuxième vertu*, 1911, in Oeuvres Poétiques complêtes (Paris: 1957) p. 527-670

Powers Erickson, Kathleen, *At Eternity's Gate: The Spiritual Vision of Vincent Van Gogh* (Grand Rapids: 1998)

Prickett, S., *Theology 80* (1977), 403-410

Rank, Otto, *Art and the Artist* (New York: 1989)

Ravasi, Gianfranco, *Il Libro Dei Salmi* (3 Vols) (Bologna: 2002)

Rocchetta, Carlo, *Guarì Tutti i Malati* (Bologna: 2015)

Six, J.-F., *Itinéraire spirituel de Charles de Foucauld* (Paris: 1983)

Solzhenitsyn, Alexander, *We Never Make Mistakes: Two Short Novels* (contains Matryona's Home) (New York: 1971)

Steinbeck, John, *The Grapes of Wrath* (New York: 1939)

Steinbeck, John, *East of Eden* (New York: 1952)

Steinbeck, John, *The Log from the Sea of Cortez* (New York: 1951)

St. Thérèse of Lisieux, *Letters of Thérèse, vol II* (Washington: 1998)

Valensin, Auguste, *La Joie dans la Foi* (Paris: 1969)

Van Unnik, W.C., *Tarsus or Jerusalem: The City of Paul's Youth* (London: 1962)

Von Balthasar, Hans Urs, *First Glance at Adrienne Von Speyr* (San Francisco: 1981)

Von Balthasar, Hans Urs, *Heart of the World* (San Francisco: 1979)

Von Balthasar, Hans Urs, *Plus Loin que la Mort*, Communio no. VI, 1 1981, p. 2-5

Von Balthasar, Hans Urs, *You Crown the Year* (San Francisco: 1989)

Von Balthasar, Hans Urs, *Love Alone is Credible* (New York: 1969)

Von Balthasar, Hans Urs, *Theology and Holiness*, Communio (Winter 1987) p. 341-350

Von Balthasar, Hans Urs, *Theological Aesthetics*, 7 vols, T. & T. Clark, 1982-1989 (GL in text)

   – *Theodrama*, 5 vols, T. & T. Clark, 1990-1998 (TD in text)

   – *Theologic*, 3 vols, T. & T. Clark, 2000-2005 (TL in text)

Von Balthasar, Hans Urs, *Mysterium Paschale* (Grand Rapids: 1993)

Von Balthasar, Hans Urs, *Explorations in Theology III, Creator Spirit* (San Francisco: 1993)

Von Balthasar, Hans Urs, *The Unknown Lying Beyond the Word* in Explorations in Theology III, Creator Spirit, p. 105-117

– *The Holy Spirit as Love, Explorations in Theology III*, Creator Spirit, p. 117-135

Von Speyr, Adrienne, *Isaias*, (Einsiedeln: 1958) p. 154f

Von Speyr, Adrienne, *Apokolypse* (Johannes) (Einsiedeln: 1977)

Von Speyr, Adrienne, *John, The Birth of the Church* (San Francisco: 1994)

Wiesel, Elie, *Night* (New York: 1960)

Wiesel, Elie, *Twilight* (London: 1991)

Wright, N.T., *Paul and the Faithfulness of God* (London: 2013)

Wright, N.T., *Romans*, p. 393-770 in the New Interpreters' Bible, 10 (2002)

Made in the USA
Columbia, SC
10 May 2018